Advance Praise

"Susan's depth and breadth of real-world
unmatched. While the book ostensibly is a_
international assistance, even the paid kind. Every Peace Corps volunteer, every
international aid worker, manager, and executive of any kind — from NGO
CEOs to World Bank experts — should devour *How to Be an Amazing Volunteer
Overseas* and assign it to their teams. It will be a text in my courses. A game
changer!"
—Kim Wilson, Sr. Lecturer, Fletcher School, Tufts University

"Invaluable guidance for anyone volunteering locally or internationally. The list of
dos and don'ts paired with stories is a great way to share important experience —
authentic, not theoretical."
—Wanjiku Kibui, Finance and Operations Consultant

"Susan is very frank and gives direct advice. The book is a lesson on understanding humans, on dignity, and on how to treat people that you believe need your
help. The depth of her truth forces the reader to reflect on their intentions. You
have represented us in the developing world very well."
**—Sidee Dlamini, Director of Stakeholder Management,
African Leadership University**

"This is an amazing compilation of information, personal anecdotes, real life lessons, and fun-to-read stories. You have demonstrated that you have to know your
privilege to truly set yourself in a position of service to others; that it is working
alongside communities and individuals who ultimately teach you more than you
could ever teach them."
—Elissa McCarter-Borde, CEO, Vitas Group

"Whilst COVID may have delayed some plans for potential volunteers, the human
urge to explore and contribute will still be there once the pandemic is over! I certainly plan to reference it when I talk to new potential volunteers and indeed staff
who want to take first assignments abroad."
—Sanj Srikanthan, CEO, Shelter Box

"I really appreciated the overall tone of respect and deference to the knowledge,
experiences, priorities and needs of organizations and/or peoples of the countries that we set out to 'help.' It is so important to take our cues from them and
to position ourselves 'in service' to people and communities. Despite today's
'wokeness,' the international aid industry still suffers from 'first worldism,' where
'developed' countries still play the role of experts advising the 'developing' world."
**—Ghada Jiha, Regional Gender Expert – Middle East,
UN World Tourism Organization**

"The opportunity to volunteer with global organizations is a privilege to not only
give of oneself, but to learn from local leadership and respect the wisdom to be
obtained."
—Dr Shelly Whitman, Executive Director, The Dallaire Institute

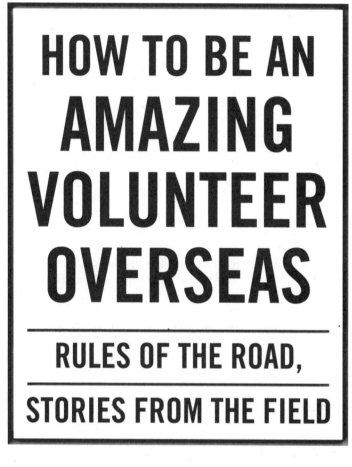

HOW TO BE AN AMAZING VOLUNTEER OVERSEAS

RULES OF THE ROAD,

STORIES FROM THE FIELD

Susan E. Gibson

With a Foreword by Nobel Peace Prize Laureate Muhammad Yunus

BARLOW BOOKS
fine books for enterprising authors

Library and Archives Canada Cataloguing in Publication data available upon
request.

978-1-988025-69-8 (paperback)

Printed in Canada

Publisher: Sarah Scott
Book producer: Tracy Bordian/At Large Editorial Services
Cover design: Paul Hodgson
Interior design and layout: Liz Harasymczuk
Copy editing: Eleanor Gasparik
Proofreading: Wendy Thomas
Indexing: Wendy Thomas

For more information, **visit www.barlowbooks.com**

Barlow Book Publishing Inc.
96 Elm Avenue, Toronto, ON
Canada M4W 1P2

In memory of my mother,
Elizabeth McPhedran Gibson.
Her encouragement of my off-the-beaten-
path life choices was the catalyst for me
to live my life with purpose.

To Professor Muhammad Yunus,
who transformed my worldview.

Net proceeds from book sales will be invested
in four education programs: in Kenya,
in Pakistan, in Bangladesh, and in
a First Nations community in Canada.

See **amazingvolunteer.com** for further information.

CONTENTS

FOREWORD

....

BY NOBEL LAUREATE PROFESSOR MUHAMMAD YUNUS

THANK YOU FOR your interest in this book. Your interest may have originated from your expressed or hidden desire to do something to make this world a better place. You have heard many stories of how individuals devoted themselves to changing people's lives, and actually succeeded in doing so. You admire these people. You feel that you are not cut out to do something as big as they have done. You think you can play only a minor role by being helpful to people who are contributing to the world, by volunteering in their work.

I want to make it very clear that these people that you admire are no different than you. In many cases, you may be in a much better position than they had been. The difference between you and them may lie in a small detail. They took one tiny step, one small unnoticeable step, in a direction different from their every-day routine steps. The departure from the routine made this big difference. A slight change of direction, over the long haul, makes you reach a destination a thousand miles away from your original destination.

Most of the time, this tiny change of direction happens in an apparently unplanned and spontaneous way. There was something in you that you were not aware of. Everyday life did not let this little something in you germinate and become visible to you. A new situation or a new experience suddenly triggers it, and you take that "spontaneous" step in a different direction. It changes your life.

People who change the world are not necessarily "special" people. They are everyday people who do not hesitate to respond to some outside signals. They deviated from their routine steps and felt happy in doing so. Once bitten by this tiny happiness, they could not resist doing it again when they saw that signal. They faced obstacles, but they could not stop. By persisting with their journey, they become the "exceptional guys" drawing admiration from the regular guys around.

Volunteering is an easy way to come closer to the people who deviate from the beaten path. Volunteering is not about discovering how these exceptional people do it; it is about discovering what you would have done in a situation like that. How would you have done it? It is about bringing yourself to a point where you feel ready to take your own first step.

This book chronicles Susan's journey to discover herself and learn to express herself in her own way. She didn't know what she was going to do, but she took the initiative to learn from others by being a part of their daily work. She chose something that intrigued her as a banker. She wanted to understand microcredit by locating herself at its place of birth, in Bangladesh, a country she did not have the slightest familiarity with. In this book, she narrates her day-to-day experiences in detail. She takes the reader with her to share her high points and low points, excitements and frustrations. Most importantly, she shares with readers what this experience meant to her.

Not everybody can jump off from her job in her home country of Canada and head for Bangladesh to find out what is going on there. For those who cannot undertake a similar journey and those who are preparing for such a courageous journey, this book will be a treasure. Don't hesitate to take this virtual journey with Susan to find out what it means to you.

You'll enjoy being a co-traveller with Susan. This experience will inspire you to unblock the part of you buried inside. This book will help you to dig it up.

Professor Muhammad Yunus
Nobel Peace Prize 2006
Founder, Grameen Bank
10 October 2020

HOW TO BE AN AMAZING VOLUNTEER OVERSEAS

INTRODUCTION

··

I **DECIDED TO** write this book to answer the many questions I repeatedly hear from students who are eager to go abroad to volunteer for the first time; from those starting a job overseas; from teachers who want to encourage young people to see the world with purpose; and from parents, who want to understand what is involved in volunteering abroad for their children.

The lure of being in the field has been a constant pull for me for 30 years. I have followed that passion by first volunteering and then working overseas in international development and microfinance roles. From 1992 to 2001, I worked in more than 40 countries as a microfinance consultant, setting up and improving programs in the Middle East, East Africa, the Caribbean, the Caucasus, and the Balkans. I have worked for Scotiabank, Save the Children, CARE, Women's World Banking, Catholic Relief Services, the US Department of State, UNHCR, UNDHA, and UNDP, as well as for the foreign aid branches of the governments of Canada, Germany, and the Netherlands. In 2001, I got married and moved to the United Kingdom and have since been involved with many non-governmental organizations (NGOs) as a board member or as an engaged donor.

When I first volunteered overseas in Haiti at the age of 30, I wanted to help people in need. I quickly realized that I wasn't adequately prepared. My first experience abroad was frustrating, exasperating, and mostly futile.

The most important point about volunteering at an NGO overseas is that you need *to learn* before you can help. It is admirable to want to give your time and energy, but gaining an understanding of a new environment is key to the outcome of your experience. Reading up on your destination prior to your departure doesn't make you an expert, but it will help prepare you for what lies ahead. It is essential not to draw conclusions about your destination and the people living there until you have first-hand experience. Once in the field, your focus should be to follow the NGO's lead, learn by doing, and share your skills when appropriate.

This book combines advice, anecdotes, excerpts from faxes, and diary entries to equip you for what to expect when volunteering overseas. It is divided into four parts: 1) deciding to go on a volunteer trip, 2) preparing to travel, 3) adapting to a new country, and 4) readjusting to life back home. Each chapter provides advice and examples from field experience.

By sharing opinions of volunteering and working abroad, I hope my book provides a productive starting point for your research. I did grapple with sharing the content of faxes to my mother and my diary entries, which weren't intended for an audience. However, I decided that if people could gain insight from my mistakes and lessons learned then it was worthwhile sharing them.

As well, my website **amazingvolunteer.com** features a selection of relevant YouTube videos of volunteers who relate their experiences in vlogs. You will also find recommended TED Talks, videos from NGOs, book suggestions, curated articles, and travel tips that could be beneficial for your research. I hope you will make the most of these online resources—they would have helped me immensely had they been available when I started out 30 years ago.

♦ ♦ ♦

In 1990, I had a strong desire to break away from my comfortable life in Toronto, Canada. Having a nine-to-five job and weekly dinners at the club was making me feel restless. Naturally, being able to forgo an income and having access to funds to hop on a plane and pay travel expenses are a necessity—which I acknowledge up front is a privilege. I was most fortunate to have supportive parents with resources who were able to fund education and travel. Also, as a white woman from a Protestant family in Canada, I was never the target of racism and didn't face obstacles to employment. I had worked at a bank for several years and in the non-profit sector for four years. I also volunteered at various community programs, which I found fulfilling.

As a next step, I wanted to venture further afield. At a local library (this was the pre-Internet era), I compiled a list of 63 organizations doing work overseas and then sent letters to them offering my services as a volunteer. I received *one* reply, from a shoestring NGO based in Toronto that supported a community in central Haiti. My goal was to help poor people in some way and gain a basic understanding of how foreign aid works, so I took the plunge. With little preparation, I departed on a three-month trip to Port-au-Prince in February 1991.

Upon arrival, I found that I had been placed at an evangelical Christian mission. I had to quickly adjust to working in an unknown environment where I didn't share the same mindset as my new colleagues since I wasn't at all religious. I was immersed in a hot and dusty rural region, face to face with extreme poverty, and I felt frustrated that the missionaries were imposing their values on local residents. My objective of helping wasn't turning out the way I had envisioned it. I thought I could arrive, roll up my sleeves, do whatever needed to be done, and everyone would be happy. It turned out to be a lot more complicated than that.

In hindsight, my first priority should have been to find an NGO that aligned with my values—this was my first and most important lesson about volunteering overseas. Nevertheless, I was determined to make the best of my time in Haiti, and despite it not being what I had hoped for, it provided invaluable lessons and a checklist of how *not* to do international development.

If I wanted to set myself up for a career in this field, it was evident that I needed to go back to school to learn about best practices in overseas service and development. In September 1991, I started a master's degree at the School for International Training (SIT) in Vermont, where I studied among like-minded people with similar goals. I was now on the right track. In addition to a basic overview of the humanitarian and emergency relief sectors, courses in intercultural communications, proposal writing, and training of trainers gave me a solid foundation for future roles in the field. Little did I know, though, that one lecture would be the turning point in my life.

We were shown an interview from *60 Minutes* (a US TV news magazine) that featured the father of microfinance and Nobel Peace Prize Laureate Professor Muhammad Yunus, an economist from Dhaka, Bangladesh. I was inspired by how Grameen Bank, founded by Professor Yunus, was making loans to poor women and getting almost perfect rates of repayment. Needing to complete the internship requirement for my degree, I immediately started plotting how I could get to Bangladesh to meet Professor Yunus.

I sent Grameen Bank a couple of faxes inquiring about an unpaid internship. When I didn't get a reply, I was not deterred. Having the means to travel overseas was clearly an advantage, so I did just that. I am a strong believer that showing up in person and meeting people face to face places you in the best position to achieve results. I was able to convince a couple of my classmates that if we could just get to Bangladesh, there would be internships for all of us. We had a Bangladeshi classmate who graciously agreed to find us a flat in Dhaka, so we decided to take a chance and set out together. Once we got to Dhaka in March 1992, I went to Grameen Bank. I told the receptionist that I was following up on faxes I had sent and was now here, ready to start. My commercial banking background along with French-to-English-translation and workshop-training experience were skills that Grameen could make use of. Luckily, Professor Yunus appreciated my determination and was kind enough to take me on. Showing up paid off!

The first thing I needed to do was to see Grameen Bank operating in the field. Arrangements were made for me to visit a rural region for a week to shadow bank workers walking from village to village, attending borrower meetings. So started my second and infinitely more productive field experience: learning the business of microfinance from the Grameen Bank staff. They instilled in me the guiding principles of what at the time was a relatively new sector in the NGO world. My three months at Grameen Bank, combined with my experience in consumer lending at Scotiabank and the skills I acquired during my master's degree, were sufficient to start a career in providing technical assistance and training in microfinance programming. I learned immensely more than I was able to contribute and am forever grateful to Professor Yunus and his staff.

The notable difference in going to Bangladesh versus my first trip to Haiti was that my purpose was to *learn*, rather than simply to volunteer. Naturally, I wanted to be helpful at Grameen Bank; I was able to make myself useful by teaching English to some of the bank's senior staff and by recording notes at international conferences. But overall, my purpose in being there was to watch and learn. As a result, my second attempt in volunteering abroad was a success, primarily because my intent had changed. I didn't know it then, but Professor Yunus would have a profound impact on my worldview. His example of challenging convention using a pragmatic approach to tackle social problems has set the benchmark for the choices I've made in work and philanthropy. Never underestimate the power of taking the initiative to meet someone you hold in high esteem—you never know how things might turn out.

❦ ❦ ❦

Whether you dream of going on an altruistic adventure, feel drawn to offer your time and skills in a new country, or need guidance in navigating the options of volunteering and learning abroad, hearing first-hand experiences can be essential in making informed decisions. You may need to fulfil a service requirement at school or complete an internship for an international studies program at university, or you may want a change from your job. This book advises you on how to get the most out of your experience and lays out some rules of the road.

At the time of writing, we are in the midst of the COVID-19 pandemic. It is clear that the world will need to adapt as the virus evolves. Ensuring that you protect your health is an additional challenge, but with advanced preparation, you can start making your plan to volunteer. I hope by the time you read this, travel restrictions are beginning to ease so that NGOs can once again welcome you.

It takes time and thoughtful planning to think through how to best participate in a new culture overseas. In order to avoid disappointment for both you and your host NGO, setting reasonable expectations from the start will contribute to a mutually beneficial learning experience. Being well prepared will significantly improve the chances of making a meaningful and fulfilling contribution—which is certainly the desired outcome.

Part 1

DECIDING TO VOLUNTEER ABROAD

YOUR MOTIVATION

The meaning of life is to find your gift.
The purpose of life is to give it away.
– PABLO PICASSO

THERE IS NO question that it is exciting to get out into the world to visit new countries, widen your perspective, and learn. The urge can be a strong one, and it can be tempting to combine it with doing something worthwhile. Volunteering abroad can be uplifting, rewarding, and life-changing—but it can also be exasperating, not what you expected, and sometimes an utter waste of time.

NINE DAYS AFTER ARRIVING IN HAITI
FAX TO: Elizabeth Gibson, Toronto, Canada
FROM: Susan Gibson, Kalico Resort, near St. Marc, Haiti
DATE: 25 March 1991

Dear Mum,
I'm looking forward to your phone call shortly. I missed you yesterday when I got sick—nothing unusual, rather typical for these parts.

I helped Rosemary, another volunteer, with the inventory of medication and supplies today. The supply room could use your organizational touch since it is an incredible mess. Various groups have donated all sorts of medicines over the years, but without first finding out what the hospital needs. As a result, there are boxes of supplies that are out of date and completely useless. I guess people think that any donation could be useful, but that is not the case.

I am starting to get an idea of how foreign aid works and it isn't as productive as I had imagined. Well-intentioned people coming for short periods of time cannot hope to accomplish much. It takes a great deal of effort and time to really understand not only the needs of the people but also their culture. I suppose that each person who comes to a developing country can at least take home a greater comprehension of the problems—but I do find it rather discouraging.

I feel that I can make myself useful for a few weeks but after that I really don't know. I don't share the same deeply religious convictions that the people here do. My plan is to go to Port-au-Prince on Thursday with the group and look up a contact at Grace Children's Hospital, a facility that treats tuberculosis.

I spend about US$10 a day on meals and US$5 for my bed. The mission has an impossible time making ends meet (they rely on donations for 70% of their budget) so every visitor is expected to pay their way. They do their best here and US$75 a week is reasonable.

Right now, I'm sitting on the balcony on the only comfortable chair around. It's 5:30 p.m., the sun is starting to go down, and thankfully the heat of the day is over. A goat and her kids just meandered by—it's another world. Love, Susie

VOLUNTEER ASPIRATIONS

You want to be of service and go abroad, but where do you start? I remember that feeling very well.

I had grown up in Toronto and had led a sheltered, agreeable life, but I was missing a sense of purpose. I got the travel bug at the age of 18 on a summer bike trip through Europe, which led to a backpacking trip after university, followed by a journey around Southeast Asia three years later. I loved being on the move, visiting interesting places, and meeting new people. The seeds for overseas adventure had been sown.

More importantly than solely seeking adventure, I very much wanted to be of service. During my teens, I helped out at several charities, and in my 20s, I provided literacy training and was a regular volunteer at a food bank. I enjoyed helping people but thought of volunteering as a weekly activity. While at university, I worked as a bank teller during the holidays. After getting my degree, I started my career as a loans officer at Scotiabank. It wasn't my ambition to work at a financial institution, but I didn't know what else to do.

Branch banking didn't turn out to be my passion, but it did furnish me with some valuable skills like credit assessment, loan collections, and customer service, which would prove applicable later on. However, I discovered that I could get involved with the Scotiabankers Association, which served the local community. I saw a chance to develop a program over the Christmas period using the bank's network of 200 branches in Toronto. I contacted the Salvation Army, which managed a list of families in need, and then assigned one family to each branch. Staff at each branch were asked to assemble a holiday basket with clothing, toys, and food to bring a little cheer to a family suffering through tough times. (Much as this approach still continues, if you ask any person in need, funds are the best way to provide assistance rather than things you think they might like.) Even if you are working for a commercial entity and your ideal job is still down the road, look for volunteer opportunities within your current employer's sustainability programs.

After a couple of years at the bank, I realized I would be happier working in the non-profit sector. I got a job at the Canadian Cancer Society and for two years managed a program to fly patients to treatment centres. Following that, I took a fundraising position at the United Way, a national charity that allocates funds based on the needs of each community. Working with NGOs was extremely rewarding, so it dawned on me that I could combine my love of travel with being of service. Immediately following my 30th birthday, I went to Haiti to get a taste of being in the field.

Turning your desire to volunteer into reality starts with initiative and a lot of research. If you want to find a program that is a fit for you and, equally importantly, for which you are fit in the host community, the ball is in your court.

MOTIVATION

Research begins with a look at yourself. The first step is to determine what your motivation is and to think through why you want to volunteer overseas. Your answers to two questions provide key insights.

Why Do You *Really* Want to Go Overseas and Volunteer?

•

Be honest with yourself right from the start. Your motivation will help guide you to make choices that benefit you. Being realistic about your reasons for going will make any experience immensely more useful and satisfying.

There is no point wasting your time and money to get involved with work that you aren't passionate about. And crucially, you don't want to waste the resources of a small NGO to look after you. Just as some people are good at math, art, or history, some are well suited to being of service.

You have to decide if being a volunteer is really for you at this stage. Some people aren't ready, or don't want to put themselves in unpredictable, potentially risky, and often frustrating situations far from home. Travel is a wonderful undertaking, but I wouldn't use volunteering as a means of quenching your desire to see the world. In itself, travel is a great way to expand your horizons, and you can always return to the idea of a volunteer trip later on. Serving overseas is for people who are determined to learn and be of help, not just interested in a way to tick off hours at an NGO to make your resumé seem more attractive.

Being compassionate and wanting to share your skills while getting experience overseas is perfectly reasonable. However, it is important to consider the long-term impact of volunteers spending a week or two in a community. Take, for example, teaching English, a common goal of volunteers. Think back to your school days and imagine if you had different teachers come every few weeks with no lesson plan to teach the ABCs and the "Head, Shoulders, Knees and Toes" song over and over again.

While it may be fun for a volunteer, the result is not advancing the education of local students.

If you have a parent, teacher, or friend who thinks volunteering abroad is a good idea, remember they aren't going—you are! You need to imagine how you would feel in a new country, where all your creature comforts aren't met and—horrors—you may not have Wi-Fi or AC or familiar food. Are you really ready to be helpful in arduous circumstances? Or will you be a nuisance, which is the last thing an NGO needs when its staff are trying to help people in need.

Be honest with yourself right from the start.

What Volunteering Are You Doing Right Now in Your Community?

It's always good to build upon experience that volunteering locally can provide. Before you go off to another country, it's best to take a look at what you can do at home.

Although not perceived as being as glamorous and exhilarating as going abroad, volunteering close to home could have more impact than a week-long trip to another country, without the costs or, crucially, the carbon emissions associated with flying. Addressing your carbon footprint is an important consideration if and when you fly. If you do conclude that you want to volunteer at a location requiring a flight, think about making a donation to compensate for your carbon emissions. On Expedia, you can click on Flight Terrapass to contribute to a carbon offset fund, and on most airline websites, you can make a donation to offset your flight prior to processing your payment.

If you are already volunteering locally, you will be well aware of the rewards of helping others. Naturally, there can be irritations, but by and large, being of value to a community can be very gratifying.

Volunteering teaches you the essential skills of co-operation, collaboration, and being a team player. It's an added bonus if your fellow volunteers come from different backgrounds or cultures so you learn to bridge contrasting mindsets in problem solving. It's advisable to have learned these skills closer to home, before considering an overseas placement.

If you aren't volunteering now, why not? There are so many needs in all communities. If you dream of being an overseas volunteer, start by looking at how you can be helpful in your community. It will be a hundred times more demanding to be of service in another country and in a different language, a new culture, and unfamiliar circumstances.

There undoubtedly are a myriad of NGOs and programs right on your doorstep doing inspiring work to address social issues. Ask around and find one that is in sync with your interests and then get involved. The list on the following page might inspire you.

Have you ever thought of writing letters for Amnesty International, helping to get refugees and asylum seekers acclimated with ShelterBox (Canada and UK) or the International Rescue Committee (IRC–US), becoming a Big Brother/Sister, or assembling outfits for Dress for Success? How about organizing fundraising events for an NGO that a friend or relative is involved in? Or you could always visit an elderly neighbour. You get the idea.

When tragedy strikes, such as the refugee crisis that led to the conditions in the notorious "Jungle" in Calais, France, in

2015–16 or Hurricane Maria in Puerto Rico in September 2017, the knee-jerk reaction is to try to do anything helpful at that moment. The first thing that often comes to mind is to donate food and clothes. In reality, people urgently need shelter and cash to start to rebuild their lives. Donations of food and clothing take time to ship, sort, store, and distribute, and usually do not meet the needs of the people that they are intended to help. The bottom line is: contributing to or fundraising for reputable NGOs that are on the front lines is the most effective way to be of assistance.

Volunteering is about connecting to people, being of service. Like anything, it takes practice and experience to be good at helping and working alongside people to solve problems. Despite good intentions, unless you are properly equipped, you are likely to be a hindrance rather than a help.

> *Volunteering is about connecting to people,*
> *being of service.*

VOLUNTEER LOCALLY

Here are a few ideas of places in your community where you can offer to help:

- animal shelter
- asylum seeker/refugee drop-in centre
- community garden
- conservation reserve
- disabled persons program
- food bank
- homeless shelter

- friendship centre for off-reserve Indigenous people
- hotline for modern trafficking and slavery victims
- literacy program
- mental health campaign
- retirement home
- safe house for domestic violence victims
- sports program for kids

....

It takes practice and experience to be good at helping.

LEARN, THEN HELP

The idea of being a volunteer overseas can culminate in an unrealistic fantasy of you disembarking the plane and swooping in—dressed in chinos, a multi-pocketed safari top, and aviator sunglasses—to help people. Having a good education, a comfortable upbringing, and some travel under your belt doesn't qualify you to solve problems elsewhere.

A scenario to shed some light on what could go wrong with no preparation: Imagine a typical volunteer who arrives in Kenya to "help" by teaching children in an orphanage. The volunteer does not speak Swahili, has no experience as a teacher, and has no training in how to deal with vulnerable children. In addition, the volunteer may struggle with extreme heat and will need accommodation (paraphrased from the book *Learning Service: The Essential Guide to Volunteering Abroad*, an excellent resource).

You can see how this situation is problematic on many levels. If you volunteer in another country without prior experience, lack appropriate training, and don't have a thorough understanding of complex issues, it is patronizing to think you can solve problems. And if you are not qualified in your own country to offer the service you want to provide, then why do you think you should be able to do so in another country?

However, if you shift your approach to *learning* how to be of help, the dynamic is entirely different. Contrary to thinking you know all the answers, it is best to arrive with a willingness to learn. Being self-aware means questioning your preconceived assumptions and stereotypes. Sharing skills, staying open-minded, and being receptive to seeing things in a different light are all welcome approaches the world over.

Before you volunteer in a country where there has been recent conflict or where there is an authoritarian regime, find out about the political and historical background. Otherwise, you may find yourself asking questions or making comments that, at best, are insensitive and, at worst, can traumatize survivors or get people into trouble with authorities.

A volunteer trip isn't about patting yourself on the back. Ideally, it should teach you what can be achieved in education, health, social justice, or other areas of community service. Volunteering overseas can have a deep-rooted impact on how you see the world and will leave a lasting impression. Once you have experimented with one trip, you can decide if you want to further your education and commitment to the sector, or if you merely want to chalk it up as a worthwhile experience.

Share skills, stay open-minded, and be receptive.

EDUCATE YOURSELF

I naively rushed off to Haiti where my goal was simply to help. In the pre-Internet days, I wasn't able to get any information in advance about the NGO to which I was being assigned. I thought I would figure things out once I got to my destination. Nowadays, there is no excuse not to do a sufficient amount of research before you go.

When I arrived in central Haiti, the basic accommodation was quite a shock. On the second floor of a cinder-block structure with a corrugated iron roof open to the elements was a dormitory with ten army cots. On the first night, I caught sight of what I thought was a kitten perched up on the rafter. When I mentioned it to one of the missionaries on the cot beside me, she laughed and said it was a rat. Having a mosquito net was a necessity for protection, not only from bug life but also from rodents roaming around at night.

At my orientation with the pastor in charge, it became clear that the NGO where I had agreed to be a volunteer was at its core proselytizing. Everyone at the mission asked me, "What are you?" I had no idea at first what they meant. Aside from being a straight white woman from Toronto, I didn't know what they were fishing for. Personality traits or my profession? No. They wanted to know my religion. I replied that I was agnostic but had grown up going to an Anglican church. This revelation proved troubling for them, and they all said they would pray for me to be saved. The goal of the mission was to convert people to Christianity, so having a volunteer who wasn't with the program was an issue. Any local resident wanting to attend the mission's school or visit the doctor at the rudimentary clinic was required to be a born-again Christian.

The reality of my experience wasn't at all what I had pictured. The ideology of the mission didn't mesh with how I wanted to help. To make matters worse, I was assigned to write up inventories of container loads full of cast-off clothing and damaged office furniture, as well as organize shelves filled with outdated medication. My contribution felt futile and had minimal, if any, positive impact. My vision of being a useful volunteer amounted to days of being exasperated and feeling like I'd not accomplished anything worthwhile for anyone.

After five weeks, I parted ways with the mission and travelled back to Port-au-Prince, where I ended up at Grace Children's Hospital, which cared for tuberculosis patients. It also had a Christian ethos, but the hospital was open to anyone who needed treatment regardless of religious affiliation. I was able to salvage my trip by volunteering for the accounting department, which was a better fit for my skills. I witnessed what an NGO with a purpose that I respected could achieve. I adopted a daily routine at the hospital and, after a short break back in Canada, returned to Haiti for an additional month to continue in my accounting role. It was fulfilling to be of service and, likewise, to feel that my contribution was valued.

Knowing what I know now, I could have saved myself 35 days of frustration had I had the courage and conviction to leave my first Haitian posting with appropriate notice. If you know that a placement is not for you, it is better to offer notice and leave, rather than waste your time—and the NGO's. Read reviews and gather advance information to identify a good NGO fit.

Read reviews and gather advance
information to identify a good NGO fit.

LEARNING SERVICE OR CULTURAL EXCHANGE TRIPS

If I could do things over, I would first invest in a structured learning trip or a cultural exchange program to get started on the right foot. Thirty years ago, I wasn't aware of educational trips on offer. Nowadays, there are an enormous number of NGOs and intermediary operators that offer placements with the goal of educating participants in how to be of service.

It takes time to think about what you actually want to get out of an experience and how you can match your skills to really be of help. The more you can learn at the beginning of the process, the better. The International Citizen Service (ICS) in the UK has developed a useful checklist about responsible volunteering (see Appendix 1).

These days, there are many intermediary operators who are in the market to plan volunteer experiences, and as the list of benefits on the following page indicates, they do offer advantages. The main criteria for selecting an operator should be that it puts the needs of a local NGO before your own.

"Voluntourism" is a profitable industry. According to the Center for Social Development's research brief, an average of close to one million Americans volunteered overseas annually during the period 2004–2014. With this level of demand, there are some unscrupulous intermediary operators that have jumped on the bandwagon to capitalize on the good intentions of idealistic travellers, while offering little practical assistance to local NGOs. If an operator promises a program including a late-morning start, a surf break, and some sightseeing thrown in, it's a sign that the operator is more interested in collecting your fee rather than prioritizing the needs of a local NGO. While reputable operators offer quality experiences, beware of those that don't have references for their placements.

Do your homework before signing up. You want to make sure that a program that looks appealing is transparent about what is being presented. Have your antenna up and check an independent source for a reference before paying for anything.

An NGO that offers short-term travel experiences and that promotes its program as a cultural exchange rather than service work is being honest in conveying that volunteers will gain as much from the host community as they will contribute. Setting up expectations that an international visitor is coming to save or serve through a short travel stint is unfair to all involved. However, due to the resources required and experience needed to host volunteers coming from abroad, many community-based NGOs aren't able to provide positions.

Do your homework before signing up.

....

BENEFITS OF USING AN INTERMEDIARY OPERATOR

An intermediary can give you access to
- Vetted NGOs: instead of starting from scratch, a list of NGOs that can accommodate volunteers—but you still should check them out for yourself

- Alumni: people who have participated in the program—interview some to see if it is a good fit for you
- Logistics: guidance on making travel arrangements
- Preparation how-to: briefing on what you need to do in advance
- Community: working alongside a group of like-minded people

Building Abroad

·

Many students are attracted to short-term trips that involve construction, or other forms of physical labour, in "exotic" countries. The underlying reason for recruiting foreign inexperienced volunteers is to bring revenue to the NGO and local community. Opportunities to engage in physical-labour tasks such as building provide volunteers with something tangible and rewarding to do while they are on a short trip, without the complexities of other types of service work that would be limited by language or cultural barriers and a short time frame. Certainly, this can be a legitimate way to raise much-needed funds.

Habitat for Humanity is an example of an NGO that uses this model successfully and is transparent about what a visitor will be doing. Their website states that they offer volunteer trips to enable travellers to immerse themselves in a new culture, while providing opportunities to build homes and experience local cultures. Volunteers join Habitat trips and, under guided supervision by skilled leaders, build homes in partnership with the local population.

WARNING ABOUT VOLUNTEERING AT ORPHANAGES

Daniela Papi-Thorton, co-author of *Learning Service: The Essential Guide to Volunteering Abroad*, who worked at the Skoll Centre for Social Entrepreneurship warns:

> In Cambodia, orphanage volunteering has become a big business. While the number of orphans has decreased, the number of orphanages has risen with the rise of tourism. UNICEF estimates that three out of every four children in Cambodian orphanages actually have one or more living parents. The most corrupt orphanage managers even have an incentive to keep children looking poor, because as I have heard many travellers say, tourists often want to give their time and money to the poorest looking place as they think that is where the most need is. People often say, "Doing something is better than doing nothing." But it isn't. Not when something is often wasteful at best and at worst is causing harm. (Source: *BBC News Magazine*, 1 May 2013)

There are many unethical people looking to take advantage of travellers wanting to do good. This is especially true if you are already on the road. You must do your due diligence by investigating any operator to ensure that its activities are legitimate and that they are actually helping the people they say they are.

RULE #1: DO NO HARM

Good intentions can sometimes have unintended negative consequences. Your actions could inadvertently do harm to the very people you are trying to help. Consider if your action is really benefiting the people you want to help. How will they feel when you go?

It may make you feel good to play with a child in tough circumstances, but what might a child go through after you leave? Children can easily become attached, so your short visit is likely to emphasize what it is a child is actually missing. If you want to truly be of help to vulnerable children, you can find ways to assist that don't negatively impact them. Volunteering for an orphanage is particularly fraught with issues—beginning with the vulnerable children, whose needs should be of paramount importance.

It is easy to have our egos wrapped up in volunteering. It is important to remember the purpose of service is about giving, contributing, and helping alongside local community members: volunteering is not about your self-importance!

KEY POINTS
1. Start by volunteering locally.
2. You need to learn before you can help.
3. Consider a learning service or cultural exchange trip.

Check out the website *amazingvolunteer.com*

To begin your research, the following links are a good starting point:

1. Watch the video "How Can I Do Good in the World?" (Learning Service, 2014). It contains tips on how to be an impactful volunteer.

2. Have a laugh watching a parody of an ill-prepared volunteer do what you *shouldn't* do in the video "Think Before You Volunteer" (VSO in Cambodia, 2019).

3. Find out how you do in the "What is your ecological footprint?" quiz.

YOUR INSPIRATION

Real change, enduring change, happens one step at a time.
– RUTH BADER GINSBURG

IDENTIFYING A LEADER who inspires you in a sector that awakens your interest is a great way to give your research direction. Follow them on social media and even make it a goal to meet in person—which may not be as implausible as it sounds. If you share the same passion and are pursuing it, there is a likelihood that your paths could cross. Leaders always want to encourage like-minded people to pursue their dreams. Naturally, accomplished people who have acquired a level of celebrity are more elusive to meet one-on-one, but don't be put off from trying. Keep track of events or conferences where they are speaking or be on the lookout for appearances at universities. Book signings are a great place to meet people. If resources permit, ideally make a plan to get to the field to visit the program or enterprise that your role model created so you can directly learn from it. That is pretty much what I opted to do.

FINDING A ROLE MODEL

In September 1991, my worldview was completely transformed. I was 30 years old, at grad school in Vermont, when I first watched Professor Muhammad Yunus being interviewed on *60 Minutes*. A social entrepreneur, banker, economist, and civil society leader from Dhaka, Bangladesh, Yunus had pioneered a new way of tackling poverty using *microcredit*—providing small unsecured loans to poor people. He had created a lending institution called Grameen Bank ("gram" means village in Bangla), and it was remarkable to see how his staff treated the clientele of poor, illiterate women with respect. The relationship between bank staff and clients was an equal partnership: clients were borrowing money with interest, so staff had to be responsive to their needs.

Yunus didn't believe that charity was the answer to poor people's problems. He saw that charity creates dependency. He wanted to use a business model that was *sustainable* in the long term to serve clients, and he succeeded. Grameen Bank has a billion-dollar loan portfolio with nine million borrowers throughout Bangladesh and a 98.9% repayment rate.

I was inspired by Yunus's vision of lending money so that people could play an active role in helping lift themselves out of poverty, while maintaining their dignity. As part of my course work for my master's degree, I was required to complete an internship in the field. I was determined to get to Dhaka to learn first-hand from the father of microfinance and understand how he was achieving such impressive results.

Meeting and learning from Yunus was a life-changing experience for me. In 1991, some questioned my aspiration to go to Bangladesh. I thought if Yunus was having such an impact, why shouldn't I go and see if I could learn from him? Taking the initiative when there was no guarantee of what the outcome would be was a chance worth taking. Even if I couldn't meet him, I thought I could learn something worthwhile along the way. Turning up on the doorstep of Grameen Bank was somewhat nerve-racking, but I was lucky that the plan succeeded. It ended up launching my career in international development. While this strategy worked in the early 1990s, I'm doubtful it would have the same result today. Nowadays, people are infinitely more accessible via e-mail, phone, and social media in every country. Don't leave your plans to chance—have your plans confirmed in advance.

Connecting to Yunus, the founder of both the microfinance and social business movements, gave me the confidence to believe that I could follow his example and help make loans available to poor people. The most important thing Yunus taught me was to put the needs of the clients first. This advice has helped me navigate challenging work situations throughout the years. By always considering the needs of the people you serve, you can maintain your focus without getting sidetracked by competing demands. Finding, then establishing, a relationship with a person who inspires you can be the start of a stimulating journey.

A FORTUITOUS ENDING

DIARY ENTRY: 15 JULY 1992 – DHAKA, BANGLADESH. It was an exceptional day! I had my wrap-up meeting with Prof. Yunus. During our conversation, I noticed a letter with the Scotiabank logo sitting on his desk. I was curious about the letter since I had worked for the bank. I was most intrigued to find that it contained a request to send a bank representative to learn about the Grameen model. I said that this was astonishing given that my understanding of the bank was to maximize profit, but Yunus said the letter was an indication that someone was thinking differently. He then gave me a copy of the letter and suggested that I contact Calum Johnston, Executive VP of International Banking, as soon as I got back to Toronto.

Two days later, on 17 July, I was back in Toronto and called Johnston at Scotiabank's head office. My father, who died in 1988, had had a long career at the bank, so I introduced myself as Douglas Gibson's daughter. I mentioned I had also worked for the bank and that I had just come from Bangladesh where I had been doing an internship at Grameen Bank. It had been Yunus's advice that I inform Johnston about my connection to the bank both through my job and my father; he said stating those facts would make bank staff feel comfortable since people are more open to a new idea from a messenger where there is common ground.

I was fortunate to have a link through my dad, but it was my first-hand knowledge of Grameen Bank that was of interest to Johnston. After our meeting, he offered me a contract to prepare a feasibility study and business plan for a microfinance program that Scotiabank could implement at one of the branches in the Caribbean.

Getting the Scotiabank contract was a big relief, given that I was down to CA$200 in my bank account when I arrived home. Being employed by the bank in an area where I had a passionate interest was something I wouldn't have thought possible. Following up on that single letter sitting on Yunus's desk paid off handsomely and set the course for my career in microfinance.

THE GRAMEEN BANK STORY

Charity only perpetuates poverty. – MUHAMMAD YUNUS

Unlike many well-intentioned international agencies donating to beneficiaries, the structure of Grameen Bank is not a top-down organization. Rather, the bank is field-led, with loan officers in villages providing services to clients working in tiny home-based businesses such as rearing poultry, sewing fishnets, and husking rice. The idea of having local bank staff make loans to poor women was groundbreaking. Poor women were respected as clients, just as the clients I had served at Scotiabank were—these clients happened to be poor people with no collateral. Small amounts of capital were improving the quality of their lives and they were able to repay the loans—it was a win-win model.

Yunus was awarded a Fulbright scholarship to study at Vanderbilt University in Tennessee. He received his PhD in 1971, the year of Bangladesh's independence. He returned to Bangladesh, and during the famine in 1974, he established a poverty-reduction program at the University of Chittagong. Having learned about trickle-down economics in the United States—and how little actually trickled down to low-income workers—he wanted to shift his focus from a macro perspective to one where he could learn how to help at a village level. In fact, in his own words, the "village women would become my teachers," which led him to develop the revolutionary model of microlending. He asked a group of women making baskets why they were so poor—thinking if people worked hard, they would earn sufficient income to feed their families. However, for a day's labour, the women would receive only enough rice to feed their families—enough to entice them back to work the following day, but never enough to break out of the cycle of poverty.

Yunus asked whether they would get a fair price if they could sell their baskets in the marketplace themselves. They said they certainly could, but they lacked working capital to buy the raw materials required to make baskets. Incredibly, the amount needed to buy straw for 42 women was a total of US$26, less than a dollar each. Yunus decided to lend, not give, them the money out of his own pocket. Within two weeks, having sold their baskets at the market, they were able to fully repay their loans. Encouraged by the result, Yunus approached a bank and proposed that they extend credit to women microentrepreneurs.

Bank personnel thought this a ridiculous notion, saying that the village women were not creditworthy since they had no collateral. Yunus felt this was unjust and replied, "Banks aren't people-worthy," and went on to establish Grameen Bank.

These millions of small women entrepreneurs with their millions of small pursuits can add up to the greatest development wonder. – **MUHAMMAD YUNUS**

Grameen Bank is based on the premise that credit is a fundamental human right for all. Typically, working capital loans are for buying cows or starting small businesses—like setting up a grocery stall at home or becoming the local "phone" lady, all of which cater to women living and working at home in villages. Previously, these women were overlooked for any loans except from the usurious loan sharks who charged exorbitant interest rates. With the arrival of Grameen Bank—and subsequent replicators—loans were offered at reasonable rates of interest. In this way, villagers had the opportunity to increase their income, thereby raising the standard of nutrition, health care, and education for their families.

As a lender, how did Yunus deal with the challenge of protecting each loan? The answer came in the form of a group guarantee—a social collateral. Any woman wanting to borrow money had to join with four other women to form a group of five. A local bank worker would organize meetings in villages for prospective clients and would explain that each group member would receive a loan to invest in her own activity. Loans would be guaranteed by all the others in a group and payments would be collected from each group, not individually. If one member wasn't able to pay, the other group members would have to cover the payment. Members therefore had to carefully select who they were willing to trust to invite into their group.

The key to the bank's overall success was that Yunus involved his target client group—poor women—and listened to their needs. Yunus solicited ideas from some of his first clients as to how they themselves could address their daily challenges. Village women created the "16 Decisions" that would, and continue to, be recited before each weekly meeting. Some of the decisions include build pit latrines (sanitation), plant trees (environment), and establish schools for children (education). These decisions are repeated before payments are collected, to reinforce what clients can do for themselves (empowerment).

Yunus incorporated their ideas into the DNA of the bank's operations. Some observers have commented that clients act like an army reciting these slogans, to which Yunus has replied,

"We are fighting a war on poverty." Clients were *stakeholders* in the process of building the bank's foundation. Exceptionally, Yunus appointed nine landless, illiterate women clients to the bank's board, so that the bank remained truly accountable to its client base. With their input, the bank was able to create other services to continue serving their clients' needs.

Grameen Bank has gained worldwide recognition with a repayment rate of almost 99% using a self-sufficient model of delivery. Its philosophy of development is based on the principle of compassion, not charity. Using business principles to sustain the model, it attracted investment—first from the donor community and then from the private sector. This formula has been reproduced in every country around the world to tackle poverty.

Changes are products of intensive efforts. – **MUHAMMAD YUNUS**

In 2006, Yunus, along with Grameen Bank, was awarded the Nobel Peace Prize "for efforts through microcredit to create economic and social development from below." The Nobel Committee said, "Lasting peace cannot be achieved unless large population groups find ways in which to break out of poverty" and that "across cultures and civilizations, Yunus and Grameen Bank have shown that even the poorest of the poor can work to bring about their own development." Yunus identified a need, which he was able to address with a business model. He didn't set out to create a bank, but his actions of lending from his own resources evolved into a sustainable large-scale enterprise. Yunus's achievement is a concrete example of what is possible for a person to accomplish. He has been able to do extraordinary things by listening to and understanding the people he believed deserved a chance to improve their circumstances.

Leading on from microfinance, Yunus continued to solve social problems using business models. In addition to Grameen Bank, he has established more than 50 businesses. One example is Grameen Shakti, a rural power company whose purpose is to supply renewable energy to unelectrified villages, as well as to create jobs. In excess of two million solar panels have been installed in villagers' homes since 1996, making it the largest home solar panel company in the world.

Yunus is on a quest to persuade business leaders around the world to set up divisions within their companies to address social problems. McCain Foods, based in Canada, accepted the challenge by creating Campo Vivo in Colombia. When the coffee market fell, local farmers were desperate to find an alternative crop. McCain staff consulted with farmers and together agreed that potatoes would be a suitable crop for the local soil. The mission of Campo Vivo is to improve the livelihoods of local farmers and their families living in low socio-economic communities: it does so by making the farmers stakeholders in the production process through to commercialization.

At its core, a social business is set up to solve a specific problem to benefit poor or disadvantaged members of society. A social business operates like a company, with the exception of not deriving profit for shareholders. Unlike a charity, which is dependent on fundraising, a social business generates profit and aims to be financially self-sustaining. A social business reinvests profits back into generating sustainable social impact. One hundred per cent of the company's profit is invested into continuing the company's social mission. It is another momentous vision that Yunus has been able to implement using a business approach, focusing on improving countless lives rather than solely making profits for shareholders.

KEY POINTS

1. People living in poverty deserve dignity and respect.
2. Listen to what local people say they need—don't make assumptions.
3. Charity creates dependency—a sustainable business model will provide clients with ongoing services they need.

Check out the website *amazingvolunteer.com*

1. If you haven't heard Muhammad Yunus speak, start with his commencement address at UC San Diego in 2016 (University of California Television).
2. Watch Devex's video "Muhammad Yunus Explains the Social Business Model & His New Book: A World of Three Zeros" (2017).
3. Take a look at the heading entitled "Where You Can Find Inspiration" to learn about people making differences in their communities around the world.

WHERE TO START

If I cannot do great things,
I can do small things in a great way.
– DR. MARTIN LUTHER KING JR.

THERE ARE TENS of thousands of inspiring community activists around the world. In order for a community or movement to succeed, it requires a leader. The secret ingredient in creating a movement for change is having someone to look up to who has a vision and commands respect. NGOs worldwide are started by people who have ideas to solve problems. However, meaningful change must have the face of a local community member taking the lead for the work to endure.

Kennedy Odede is one such man. Many of us can't imagine achieving anything as remarkable as he has (see profile on following page). While being an exceptionally inspirational leader, he would be the first to tell you that he could never have succeeded without the participation of the Shining Hope for Communities (SHOFCO) team and the support of community members.

Volunteers can be very helpful in supporting the vision of local pioneers and advancing the mission of NGOs.

PROFILE OF A GRASSROOTS LEADER: KENNEDY ODEDE

Kennedy Odede from Kibera, Nairobi, in Kenya is a community activist in his mid-30s. At age 16, he was working at a factory on the outskirts of Nairobi, earning just US$1 per day. Having read Martin Luther King Jr.'s biography, he was inspired by what King had been able to achieve. An initiator rather than a follower, Odede saw the potential for change in his community. But where do you start tackling the challenges in Africa's largest slum? Odede instinctively knew that energy is created when you unite people toward shared goals. He came up with the idea of bringing young people together through sport. With 20 cents, he bought a soccer ball—and that one small action was the genesis of an NGO called SHOFCO.

Despite starting out with challenges that many would consider insurmountable, Odede had hope and determination that he channelled into action. He successfully built a team of fellow residents who together worked with the community at large, all committed stakeholders in the programs they have developed and continue to maintain and grow. Given that the government routinely ignores slums, SHOFCO has taken the initiative to partner with countless community members and groups as well as international donors. This formula is producing significant results in improving the lives of many. SHOFCO now employs 500+ local staff members and provides residents with potable water, education for girls, and many other programs and services that Odede himself lacked growing up. SHOFCO works in more than 15 informal settlements in Kenya and serves in excess of one million people. The team at SHOFCO has made significant strides in addressing long-term systemic problems.

Beating the odds, Odede has devoted his life to lifting others out of poverty, and he is a beacon for many young people aspiring to build better lives. He has been acknowledged by many organizations worldwide, including by the World Economic Forum as a Young Global Leader and by the Obama Foundation as one of their African Leaders in 2018.

AN INTRODUCTION TO THE NGO WORLD

Before you go full steam ahead into researching specific NGOs that sound interesting, it is advisable to have a basic overview of the sort of work done in the international development and the humanitarian sectors. Recognizing the differences between distinct sectors and which NGOs do what will help you in your search.

Saying that you want to volunteer for the United Nations (UN) is not only extremely vague, it is not a feasible option. If you do want to be of service to UN agencies or humanitarian NGOs in a professional capacity, you will need to train and qualify to be considered for postings. Getting experience by first volunteering overseas will help you decide if this is an avenue you want to pursue professionally.

Given that my background was in economic development and education, I am sticking to examples in the international development sector. However, you can follow the same principles of researching NGOs that I outline if your interest lies in other areas such as climate change, wildlife, or environmental conservation.

Humanitarian Work vs. International Development
•

Work in the humanitarian world is often short term and governed by principles of humanity, neutrality, impartiality, and independence. Humanitarian efforts are designed to alleviate suffering and maintain and protect human dignity in the aftermath of a disaster, be it man-made or a natural catastrophe. Because we see images of natural disasters and conflicts in the news, they tug at our heartstrings. It is no wonder that volunteers want to rush to sign up to help NGOs that assist people in crises. However, this sort of work is emergency in nature, so highly skilled and trained personnel are required. Needless to say, most NGOs working in dangerous areas simply don't have the capacity to take on inexperienced volunteers, who also take up valuable resources like accommodation and food provisions in short supply during times of crises. Some NGOs like Médecins Sans Frontières/Doctors Without Borders and ShelterBox accept volunteers, but a year's training is required before joining a response roster.

Imagine if a house is on fire, it would be unthinkable for an untrained person to bolt into the flames without proper training and gear. The bottom line is that your compassion alone doesn't qualify you to help out in emergency situations.

But don't be dismayed! There are lots of opportunities in the international development sector. When you think about the underlying causes of poverty, what comes to mind? In essence, it boils down to people lacking access to water, food, shelter, health care, education, sanitation, and infrastructure. NGOs around the world are working to address the enormous challenges faced globally by two billion people who live in extreme poverty, existing on less than US$2 per day.

CHOOSING AN NGO AND REGION

Choices abound. The first step is to decide where you'd like to go. Your destination may be because of an inspiring leader you have read about or perhaps you would like to visit a geographic region with which you have an affinity or family heritage. Identify a sector that matches your interests and then focus your research on NGOs working within that sector. For each NGO that catches your attention, find out its aims and objectives, then determine if they align with yours. It is useful to know when an NGO was established, what it has achieved, and its sources of funding. These points give you important information about an NGO's impact and track record in partnering and sustainability.

Identify a sector that matches your interests.

Websites like Charity Navigator and GuideStar are good tools for confirming that an NGO you are considering is reputable and doesn't spend an inappropriate percentage of funds on its administration costs. When I was researching NGOs in 1990, Google didn't exist but now it is incredibly easy to get key facts.

Once you have a first-round list of NGOs, get in touch with representatives to ask about the recruitment procedure for volunteers. Also request introductions to former volunteers so you can find out about their experiences.

A lot of NGOs quite rightly charge volunteers; it is an important source of funds to help provide support for your orientation, supervision, and accommodation. Finally, you should make sure you are interviewed and vetted, which also gives you the opportunity to confirm that you connect with the values of the NGO. The process is much like dating—if at all possible, try to avoid blind dates.

Confirm that you connect with the values of the NGO.

FRAMING YOUR NGO SEARCH

Further insight into the NGO world comes from an important list related to international development goals that provide overall context. Within each goal, there are countless subsectors, all of which aim to improve the lives of all people. It is important to note that the list neglects mental health and disability, areas that also deserve much attention.

Sustainable Development Goals

•

The 17 Sustainable Development Goals (SDGs) were adopted in September 2015 by the UN General Assembly to create a better world by 2030. Detailed descriptions are included at **amazingvolunteer.com**, but here is a brief summary:

1. To **end poverty**
2. To **end hunger**, achieve food security and improve nutrition, and promote sustainable agriculture
3. To ensure **healthy lives** and promote well-being
4. To ensure inclusive and equitable **quality education** and promote lifelong learning opportunities
5. To achieve **gender equality** and empower all women and girls
6. To ensure availability and sustainable management of **water and sanitation**
7. To ensure access to affordable, reliable, sustainable, and **modern energy**
8. To promote sustained, inclusive, and **sustainable economic growth** and decent work
9. To build **resilient infrastructure**, promote inclusive and sustainable industrialization, and foster innovation
10. To **reduce inequality** within and among countries
11. To make cities and **human settlements inclusive**, safe, resilient, and sustainable
12. To ensure **sustainable consumption** and production patterns
13. To take urgent action to combat **climate change** and its impacts
14. To conserve and **sustainably use the oceans**, seas, and marine resources for sustainable development
15. To protect, restore, and promote sustainable use of **terrestrial ecosystems**; sustainably manage forests; combat desertification; and halt land degradation and biodiversity loss
16. To promote **peaceful and inclusive societies** for sustainable development; provide access to justice for all; and build effective, accountable, and inclusive institutions at all levels

17. To strengthen the means of implementation and revitalize the **global partnership** for sustainable development

Millennium Development Goals
·

The SDGs followed the eight Millennium Development Goals (MDGs) agreed on by world leaders at a UN summit in 2000:

1. To eradicate extreme poverty and hunger
2. To achieve universal primary education
3. To promote gender equality and empower women
4. To reduce child mortality
5. To improve maternal health
6. To combat HIV/AIDS, malaria, and other diseases
7. To ensure environmental sustainability
8. To develop a global partnership for development

IN THE BEGINNING: THE UNIVERSAL DECLARATION OF HUMAN RIGHTS

Eleanor Roosevelt was a driving force in creating the Universal Declaration of Human Rights. Following the horrors of the Second World War, together with John Peters Humphrey and René Cassin, Eleanor played an indispensable role in drafting the milestone document that set out a common standard of achievements for all peoples and all nations.

Eleanor and her husband, Franklin D. Roosevelt, arrived in the White House in 1933 as First Lady and President. Deeply committed to human rights and social justice issues, Eleanor was an advocate of equal rights for women, African Americans, and Depression-era workers. In 1946, she was appointed as a delegate to the UN by President Harry Truman, who succeeded President Roosevelt after his death in 1945.

As head of the Human Rights Commission, Eleanor mustered support for the adoption of the Universal Declaration of Human Rights, which she submitted to the UN General Assembly. She famously said: "We stand today at the threshold of a great event both in the life of the United Nations and in the life of mankind. This declaration may well become the international Magna Carta for all men everywhere." (In the final document "men" was replaced by "human beings.")

President Truman referred to Eleanor as "First Lady of the World" for her lifelong humanitarian achievements. With her persistent determination and dedication, systemic change became achievable. The Declaration provided the foundation for the subsequent MDGs and SDGs—which have become the international framework for NGOs in their mission to improve lives around the world.

KEY POINTS

1. Determine which international development area appeals to you.
2. Research NGOs in the sector that spark your interest.
3. Familiarize yourself with the SDGs, and the Universal Declaration of Human Rights.

Check out the website *amazingvolunteer.com*

1. To learn about SHOFCO's impact in Kibera, watch "This Is SHOFCO" (Shining Hope for Communities, 2017).

2. For a quick overview of the SDGs, watch "A Look at the Sustainable Development Goals" (United Nations Foundation, 2015).

3. Watch the inspiring speech that laid the foundation for the SDGs in the video "Beacon of Hope: Eleanor Roosevelt & the Universal Declaration of Human Rights" (United Nations, 2018).

HOW TO BE USEFUL

When you talk, you are only repeating what you already know.
But when you listen, you might learn something new.

– DALI LAMA

IMAGINE YOURSELF AT an NGO overseas. Put yourself in the shoes of the director at your host NGO and try to envison what sort of qualities in a volunteer would be welcomed and appreciated. You want to put your best foot forward to make yourself useful. The skills and capabilities described on the following pages are valued in most workplaces, but particularly so in an international volunteer role.

SEE YOURSELF AS A PARTNER

Partnership is the best model to create long-term positive impact. Doing *with* others as opposed to doing *for* others is the guiding principle. The most impactful NGOs are the ones created by individuals at the grassroots of their local community, working with partners to scale up their work.

Beware that good intentions don't always lead to positive impact. Ask local staff to be your guides and try to be helpful on their terms, without taking up too much of their time. Ultimately you want to learn, be of service, and have local staff pleased to have you around. Given the onerous environments that many NGOs work in, you will face some inconveniences, so it is important that you are passionate about the NGO's work while you find meaningful ways to join in what they do.

DEFINE AND ALIGN YOUR EXPECTATIONS

Determine what you want to learn. What excites and interests you? What work could you do? Before figuring out what you are going to pack, focus on creating a list of goals and objectives for your volunteer work.

Make a list of your expectations before you go and share it with your host NGO. Prior to your departure, ask for a job description or task list: knowing your role in advance ensures that the host NGO has thought through your involvement. That way you can flag any misalignments in expectations at an early stage. Your host NGO might be able to suggest workshops or links to training that would help you come well prepared.

Flag any misalignments in expectations.

Your goal is to avoid NGO staff trying to find things for you to do. Identifying activities for unqualified volunteers takes up a lot of time, and like any NGO, they are short on resources.

LISTEN AND OBSERVE

Do you think you are a good listener? Perhaps you are, but most of us need to work—a lot!—at developing this skill. In fact, listening is more of a discipline than a skill. I can't emphasize enough how important it is to be good at hearing what people are trying to communicate to you. Listening could be the key to the success of your visit, and it will set you apart from others who love the sound of their own voices. Concentrating on what people are saying, notably in an unfamiliar situation, puts you in a good position to navigate obstacles.

Take your time to get to know your new environment. Use your powers of observation. Sometimes the best thing you can say is nothing. If you think you know the answers, your preconceived opinions won't allow you to be open to new information. Right from the start, asking questions and focusing on what your hosts say will open lots of doors and people will be receptive to you. It is a good policy to keep your views to yourself and let others tell you what they think. In his book *The 7 Habits of Highly Effective People: Powerful Lessons in Personal Change*, author Stephen Covey summarizes it well: "Most people do not listen with the intent to understand; they listen with the intent to reply."

Take your time to get to know your new environment.

Differences in communicating and language barriers may not be evident at first. Staff at your host NGO will naturally want you to feel welcome. If they do not understand something you've said, they will go to great lengths not to offend you. Visitors usually look for acknowledgement to make sure their message is understood, but often a local person will reply affirmatively since they don't want you to take offence. An example of a possible exchange: You ask, "Do you have an adapter I could borrow?" and the person replies, "Yes" with a big smile but doesn't give you an adapter.

When you arrive, it can be easy to view things in a simplified way. Resist any temptation to say, "All you need to do is..." and offer solutions. Your hosts have been living in their environment for a long time. It is important to listen to the history and understand what has been done to address issues—it is never as straightforward as you might think.

Rather than identifying solutions, find out what the NGO's priorities are. Having the space and time to think aloud with a volunteer can be beneficial for the NGO, but as a volunteer, it is important to support their solutions.

ATTITUDE IS EVERYTHING

In addition to being a good listener, having patience is more than a virtue as a volunteer. When things don't go your way, take a deep breath to help you stay calm and grounded. Arm yourself with compassion and understanding. Most often you will be working with a team: accepting that people have different working styles is key. Try not to be judgmental. If a new colleague has an approach that differs from yours, find out why and be open to learn an alternative method of tackling a task.

Arm yourself with compassion and understanding.

Take initiative when appropriate and be adaptable when things don't pan out in your favour. Amazing volunteers are passionate about wanting to get work done, without making a fuss or worrying about taking credit.

SHARE YOUR SKILLS

There are a multitude of NGOs in many countries where you can volunteer in a relatively safe environment. Giving up your time and going to another part of the world to contribute your knowledge and skills can be commendable, but the onus is on you to prepare and choose an NGO that lines up with your values and passion.

Focus on sharing your skills rather than giving away money or things. The act of giving material objects can boost your ego, but sharing resources is more constructive for recipients. The outdated model of Western volunteers giving things to indebted recipients in the developing world isn't sustainable or empowering. If you feel you have little to learn and a lot to give, you risk becoming a new-age colonialist!

Take a look at the list on the following page, which notes skills that are most helpful to NGOs. By highlighting where your areas of expertise are a good match, you will enable an NGO to see where you might best fit in.

If you haven't yet had relevant work experience, start off with a learning trip or cultural exchange. This will help you determine where you want to direct your future volunteering. If you are not qualified for a position in your country, most likely you will not be qualified in your host country either (e.g., teaching or working with vulnerable children). And although having a driver's licence can be useful, for insurance reasons, you won't be able to drive a vehicle owned by an NGO.

If you have a particular skill, look for ways not just to provide it but also to transfer it to someone locally. This will enhance your contribution, enabling it to live on when you leave.

....

HELPFUL SKILLS FOR NGOS

- accounting and budgeting
- advocacy and policy work
- agribusiness: land use, crops, livestock, soils, wells, dams
- computing and coding
- early childhood education
- environment and conservation
- food security and distribution
- fundraising
- governance
- human resource management
- language training (TOEFL)
- legal services
- logistics and delivery systems
- marketing and communications: social media, videography, photography
- medicine, nutrition, and public health
- proposal development, grant writing, and editing
- psychology, therapy, social work
- safety and security systems

- small business: food preparation, hospitality, garment making, hair dressing/barbering
- sports, music, and art
- trades: e.g., plumbers, electricians, carpenters, painters, builders, engineering (water and sanitation)
- training and workshop planning
- translating and interpreting

SHARING AND RELAYING SKILLS

DATELINE: SEPTEMBER 2000 – BANJA LUKA, REPUBLIKA SRPSKA. On a visit to a microfinance program called Mikra, originally funded by Catholic Relief Services (CRS), I was responsible for creating a team-building workshop for program staff working throughout Bosnia and Herzegovina and Republika Srpska (RS). Given that the Bosnian War ended in December 1995, diplomacy was essential. Even though staff members in both regions were now working for the same program, they had been on opposite sides in the war. Understandably, underlying tensions remained. Both groups in the two regions shared the goal of providing service delivery to their clients, which was a good starting point.

I arrived in Sarajevo where I met with the senior management team. We visited clients to get a handle on how the program was operating and then discussed issues they wanted to address in the workshop. They had agreed to hold the workshop in Banja Luka, the main city in RS. I had worked with the team previously, so they were familiar with the participatory training approach. Together we developed objectives and activities that would appeal to and resonate with all participants. Each team member took responsibility to prepare a portion of the workshop that would take place the following day.

The workshop would be conducted in the local language. With the exception of my saying hello, there was no translation, which would allow for conversation to flow and ideas to easily be exchanged without disruption. When the workshop started, I followed the program we had prepared in English, and during breaks the team let me know how things were going and asked advice if needed. Once we got the ball rolling with some icebreakers, there was a good energy.

We started out on somewhat tricky footing and ended up at a pizzeria for dinner with everyone enjoying a meal together. Although I was at the dinner, everyone was speaking in the local language, so I just sat back and watched. I was reminded that to be successful as a catalyst, you must do all you can to pass on the baton to your local colleagues to take ownership. Taking your ego out of the equation will lead to effective local capacity building. After all, the local staff are the ones who will drive the work forward.

VOLUNTEERS WITH LIMITED EXPERIENCE

Polly Dolan, founder of the SEGA Girls Secondary School in Morogoro, Tanzania, has discovered that volunteers with limited experience can be beneficial, provided they are managed by a local staff member:

The creativity, energy, and diverse viewpoints of the many volunteers who have visited SEGA have enriched the organization for more than ten years. Every volunteer impacts the lives of our students in unique ways, leaving their mark on the school. The students at SEGA are excited to interact with volunteers coming from a variety of countries, practice English, see photos of their families and friends, and gain exposure to new ways of thinking and doing things. Volunteers have helped SEGA teachers by:

- running extracurricular activities in art, sports, and music
- assisting in organic gardening
- facilitating letter writing, video conferences, or other interactive activities between our students in Tanzania and sponsors or sister schools in the US
- capturing moments and anecdotes, and documenting day-to-day activities at the school through photos, video, and writing
- writing grants and proposals
- conducting impact evaluations

At SEGA, we are fortunate to have resources to provide a structured cultural exchange and match volunteers with activities that are managed and supervised by a staff member.

RECRUIT FINANCIAL AND MORAL SUPPORT

There are practical considerations in going overseas to volunteer in terms of your own support—both financial and moral. Decide what sort of time commitment you want to make and then calculate what budget you need to keep afloat. In 1991, when I made up my mind to volunteer in Haiti, I gave up my apartment and moved my belongings to my mother's house, leaving me with only a few financial obligations. Crucially, I also had worked for more than six years and had savings that I was willing to invest in my next chapter with the hope it would redirect my life in a positive way.

When calculating the costs of volunteering overseas, you have to factor in flights and daily living expenses. Usually, an NGO will charge a weekly fee that includes your accommodation and meals plus an additional amount to cover costs of staff members developing and supervising activities and projects for you. If an intermediary operator arranges your trip, they will have their fee included in the weekly amount. Even though you want to be helpful, resources have to be spent to look after volunteers. Many NGOs are willing to take on volunteers and have the view that by doing so, they can highlight their successes with the hope of attracting funding to their NGO.

In addition, recruit the support of your nearest and dearest. I'm forever grateful to my mother for being so encouraging of my plan to go to Haiti. Not surprisingly, there were some naysayers who thought my adventure was downright impetuous. It is natural that well-intentioned family members and friends who are themselves risk-averse will try to discourage you. They may even think you're judging them or feel your leaving is a rejection of their life choices. Don't be disheartened.

Some questions you are likely to hear: "Why go away? Isn't your life fine as it is?" and "Lots of people don't really like their jobs—you'll get used to yours" and "But I'll miss you! And you won't be here for my wedding/birthday party!"

Having a few empathetic close friends and/or family members can offset the skepticism or negativity you will no doubt encounter. My mother was continually supportive during the years when I made the transition from field volunteer to microfinance consultant. I was also fortunate to always be able to count on several good friends who cheered me on from afar.

HOW TO BEST USE YOUR TIME AND TALENTS

DIARY ENTRY: 13 APRIL 1992 – DHAKA, BANGLADESH. I like our Bangla class but know I'll have to make more of an effort to practice. I felt comfortable enough to go to the post office on my own. I had a fax from Mum and she seems fine. I'm not feeling homesick at all now; then again, I've only been gone a month. Now I have to figure out what I want to get out of my stay here.

1. Learn survival Bangla. Be able to communicate at a basic level. Attend class every day, review the lesson in the evening, and use every available opportunity to practice with native speakers at the market, etc.
2. Gain an appreciation of Bangladeshi culture and read about historical events that led to present-day Bangladesh. Visit Bangladeshis in their homes, listen to local music, and ask my students questions about their culture.
3. Study Grameen Bank's operations and see how they can be applied in other countries.
4. Learn about Grameen Bank's structure and identify strengths and weaknesses. Interview bank employees. Review existing GB material, reports, videos.
5. Assist at Grameen Bank's International Dialogue Program. Attend workshops, review project proposals submitted by organizations who want to replicate the GB model. Assist with correspondence, compile internship guidelines and expectations.

Tonight, we watched a spectacular lightning show from our rooftop. After the rain, the sounds of chickens and frogs were musical albeit very noisy.

KEY POINTS
1. Do *with* others, not *for* others.
2. Create a list of NGOs that align with your values and compile a list of your expectations.
3. Being a good listener is the key to successful communication.

Check out the website *amazingvolunteer.com*
1. Hyram, a well-intentioned young traveller, explains voluntourism and why you need to be careful in the video "I Was a Humanitarian … and I Regret It" (Selfless, 2020).
2. Answer yourself the six questions in the one-minute video "Do You Have What It Takes?" (GoAbroad.com, 2017).
3. Watch the video about the importance of effective communication, "Being a Good Listener" (The School of Life, 2016).

Part 2

PREPARING TO GO

PLANNING YOUR TRIP

Travel is fatal to prejudice, bigotry and narrow-mindedness.
– MARK TWAIN

THERE IS MUCH to do once you have landed a volunteer position at an NGO. Your host NGO is the authority, so pay attention to what they advise during your lead-up time to your visit. Your job is to do everything you can to obtain all travel documents and to sort out health requirements so that you are as ready as possible. Don't leave things to the last minute—being proactive will make the run-up to your trip less pressured.

WAR IN THE REGION: IS IT SAFE TO GO?

DATELINE: OCTOBER 1999 – SKOPJE, NORTH MACEDONIA. I was in the process of arranging a contract with CRS to implement a microfinance program. However, the NATO bombing campaign of Serbia was in full force, and Skopje Airport had been closed due to its proximity to Belgrade. CRS personnel didn't feel there was any immediate danger in Skopje, but the issue was how to get there safely. One option was flying into an airport in northern

Italy and then taking a five-hour car trip, but it meant someone would have to come and collect me. Although staff members were eager for me to get the new program up and running, we concluded it would be sensible to postpone my arrival until the airport reopened. A few weeks later, CRS called to say that the airport was back in business and that I should book my flight as soon as possible.

CONTACT YOUR HOST NGO

Once you receive confirmation that you have been accepted as a volunteer, request a briefing call with your host NGO. They are the best source of information about the country you will be travelling to and about what to expect on-site. They will also be able to give you relevant information on how to best prepare and will provide an overview of practicalities on the ground.

ASSESS POTENTIAL RISKS

Many countries where NGOs are based can be facing difficult circumstances. However, local NGO staff are accustomed to the environment and will have protocols in place to address all eventualities. A reputable NGO will not want to risk having you in the country if your security is an issue—they don't want the additional stress of worrying about you if there is real danger and will advise you accordingly. Trust the recommendations of your host NGO. Check government travel advisories regarding the country you want to travel to. A word of caution, though: if you take to heart every warning, chances are you won't even leave your house, let alone your country. You do need to inform yourself of the risks, but don't let them put you off your trip, provided your host NGO gives you the green light.

Trust the recommendations of your host NGO.

Often, seeing news reports of dangers in distant countries can leave long-lasting negative impressions. Just because there are reported issues in one part of a country doesn't mean that the entire country is affected. That being said, it is likely that an NGO where you want to volunteer is operating in a country where civil unrest or natural disasters loom on the horizon. The country will have many positive attributes, but these are not usually advertised. Just as your home country doesn't want to be known solely for, say, gun violence, racism, crime, drug use, housing shortages, or such issues, other countries shouldn't be defined by their challenges.

For volunteers without experience, it is especially important not to take unnecessary chances in areas deemed dangerous. Sadly, there are cases of well-intentioned people who desired to help and travelled to countries in the middle of a war and paid with their lives. Leave the emergency humanitarian aid in the hands of seasoned professionals and get your experience in a safer environment.

Set up a Google alert or a local news feed for the country and/or region in the months before you travel to stay informed of national and local news and what matters to local people. Becoming acquainted with the region you're going to will be very helpful as you'll realize that rather than war and disease, the locals are often more interested in football results and celebrity scandals.

Make a list of questions you have regarding security (see suggested list below) and ask your NGO for guidance, so that you are equipped to respond to family members who may be wary of your travelling to a destination unknown to them. It is important to get reliable up-to-date information in advance.

Do your due diligence on your host NGO. This will make you feel more confident about your decision and you can then concentrate on getting all the things you need to do done prior to your departure rather than worry unnecessarily.

Do your due diligence on your host NGO.

....

ASK YOUR NGO

As part of your advance research, it is perfectly reasonable to ask:
- What are the current security risks in the country?
- Are there any local issues you need me to be aware of?
- What precautions are in place at your NGO?
- Will I be travelling in-country, and if so, how?

....

IT'S ALL ABOUT PERSPECTIVE

DATELINE: APRIL 1992 – DHAKA, BANGLADESH. I arrived at Grameen Bank to start my internship one year after the 1991 Bangladesh cyclone, one of the deadliest tropical storms ever recorded. Tragically, tens of thousands of Bangladeshis in the Chittagong region on the Bay of Bengal died as a result of the catastrophic floods. Concerned family members and friends in

Canada expressed doubts about my going to a country that, in their minds, would be under water. I was going to the centrally located capital Dhaka, which didn't pose any threat to my safety. Conversely, when I was about to fly home to Canada in July 1992, the Los Angeles riots following the murder of Rodney King were raging. Television news coverage painted a terrifying scenario of LA burning and many people being killed and injured. My Bangladeshi friends were fearful that I was going to North America—clearly a dangerous place. I assured them that although the riots were of grave concern in LA, it was safe for me to return to Toronto 4,000 kilometres away.

ACQUIRE TRAVEL VISAS IN ADVANCE

Once you have your placement confirmed, ask your host NGO what visa(s) you need to travel to your destination. It is likely you will require a letter of invitation to accompany your visa application, which your host NGO can provide. It is important to follow your NGO's advice on the type of visa to apply for and what exactly needs to be written on the application form. Applying for a tourist visa when your volunteer position might be classified as work could pose an issue: be clear about your intentions with the consular department of the host country's embassy.

Make sure you check the validity of your passport as soon as you plan to go. If you are a frequent traveller, ensure you have a sufficient number of empty pages in your passport. Most countries no longer allow you to add extra pages to your passport, so if you have a lot of stamps, you may want to renew it ahead of time. Also, your passport must be valid for at least six months.

Do *not* leave getting your visas until the week prior to travel since some embassies and high commissions can take several weeks to process visas. In a pinch, you can usually pay an expedited fee or engage an agent to get a visa on your behalf, but it means spending a lot of money needlessly.

SOMEONE LEFT OUT SOME PERTINENT TRAVEL INFORMATION

DIARY ENTRY: 13 FEBRUARY 1996 – GENEVA–MOSCOW–YEREVAN. It's a grey, rainy, and raw day in Geneva. I'm excited, nervous, and anxious about my contract in the Caucasus. Everything will be new to me, but I hope that I'll be able to soak up information quickly enough to come up with sensible recommendations. The UN travel department in Geneva booked me on an Aeroflot flight to Moscow, with a connection to Yerevan, Armenia. Being airborne in a thick, bumpy cloud mass is unnerving—I hope the radar works.

I am in business class, but in reality, it doesn't equate to standard economy. The man in front of me is bouncing around constantly causing the tray table to unlatch and hit me in the face. The man behind me is smoking a cigar—there is no attempt to enforce the "no smoking" policy. I am going to pass on lunch and the entire bottle of vodka offered.

🍁 🍁 🍁

When we landed in Moscow, we waited on board for half an hour before making our way down the icy stairs. It was a perishingly cold -30 degrees Celsius. Once inside the terminal, I was informed that my connecting flight was in fact at another terminal. Furthermore, I required a transit visa and would have to pick up my luggage—so much for the promise of checking my bag through to Yerevan. I was mentally prepared for some glitches, so I went off to find the visa office. I got the transit visa I needed within 15 minutes but ended up going through the wrong passport control so I had to scout around for an English-speaking agent who could clear up the misunderstanding.

After locating my bag, an Aeroflot agent told me that my flight to Yerevan was departing from an airport 90 minutes away! That couldn't be right, so I decided to consult another agent who then reassured me that the flight was leaving from the nearby Terminal 1, and it would cost US$25 to get there. I asked for written instructions in Cyrillic, so that there would be no confusion with a taxi driver. The experience was like being on a scavenger hunt.

The waiting area at the nearby terminal was filled with people wearing fur hats and smoking incessantly; one man was reading *Playboy*. I am now sitting on a flimsy plastic chair, waiting with about 50 other passengers for passport control to open. I have a feeling I might actually get to Yerevan by 2 a.m. with my luggage. (Luckily, I did.)

BE PREPARED FOR BORDER CROSSINGS

Upon arrival in most countries, you will be required to complete a landing card. You will almost certainly be asked the address of your accommodation and the duration of your visit. Before you depart, ensure you have the name of your hotel/hostel and its street address (or at least the town it is located in). In the event you don't have the accommodation address, write down the address of the NGO's office, which you will find on your letter of invitation. It isn't advisable to tell an immigration official that you don't know where you are staying since it will result in further questions about your entry and the purpose of your visit. Also have the phone number of the person who will be meeting you, so you can text them when you land.

When travelling to countries with predominantly Muslim populations, if you have an Israeli stamp in your passport, many Muslim countries will reject your request for a visa. You can travel to Muslim countries—just make sure your passport isn't stamped in Israel—request a paper insert instead. If you already have an Israeli stamp and want to visit Arab countries, other than Jordan, Egypt, and UAE, you will need to apply for a new passport. Check restrictions before you set out since there are recent changes in the region.

Finally, take a look at a map of the region you will be travelling to in case there is a nearby country you might want to explore on the way home. Bring along extra passport photos and copies of your passport information page and birth certificate so it will be easy to apply for additional visas.

TAKE HEALTH PRECAUTIONS

Find out which vaccinations are required at your destination. In some countries, it is necessary to have a certificate confirming that you have had the yellow fever vaccination and/or proof of a negative HIV test result. Given the COVID-19 pandemic, it is likely you will also need to have proof of a recent negative test result and a vaccine certificate when available.

Schedule medical and dental checkups prior to your trip. Make sure you get a prescription for any medications you need to take with you. Ask your doctor for a letter stating the intended purpose of any prescribed drugs you will be carrying with you and keep the letter with your meds. Policies regarding controlled substances in most countries are very strict, so protect yourself in case a border control official goes through your toiletries.

At an international travel clinic, get a copy of the International Certificate of Vaccination or Prophylaxis booklet (WHO format) to keep track of shots and their expirations. Confirm that all of your basic inoculations are up to date, including tetanus, diphtheria, polio, and MMR (measles, mumps, and rubella). It is highly recommended to get shots for water-borne illnesses too, such as typhoid and Hepatitis A. From experience, without referring to a booklet, it is impossible to remember when you need which shots. On more than one occasion, I got an extra shot when I was already covered.

Regarding malaria prevention: often you will be advised to take anti-malaria tablets if a country has any cases of malaria. Ask your host NGO for advice about the region where you will be staying. When I went to Bangladesh in 1992, I was informed by a travel clinic that the country had malaria so for a hefty sum, I got tablets for the duration of my stay. It turned out that there was no malaria at all in the capital city of Dhaka, where I was based. Nor were there any cases of malaria in the areas I visited. Taking anti-malaria medication gives some people adverse side effects, so take them only if absolutely necessary.

Travellers often overlook how incredibly important dental health is, so visit your dentist before you set out. Take it from someone who ended up with a root canal issue in Georgetown,

Guyana, in 1992. Practicing dentists were few and far between in the country, and one of them was the president! I suffered for an entire week and don't want to recall the pain of the dental work that was needed upon my return.

Schedule medical and dental checkups prior to your trip.

And finally, contact an insurance agent and invest in dependable medical insurance that will protect you sufficiently. Generally, you pay up front for minor medical services and are reimbursed on your return, so keep any receipts in order to submit a claim. Ensure you are covered in the event you need to travel to a nearby country to get treatment.

Invest in dependable medical insurance.

CONSIDER COMMUNICATION ARRANGEMENTS

Make a plan to keep in touch with family members. Start with the premise that you will have limited reception on your mobile phone. If it turns out that you have high-speed Wi-Fi at your destination, you are exceptionally lucky, but don't bank on it. You will want to put your family members' minds at rest. If they don't hear from you, they will worry. Check in advance with your host NGO what options are available to maintain connectivity. Use your volunteer stint as an opportunity to go offline for a bit to connect with the people you are working with, or perhaps start a blog or write letters.

Make a plan to keep in touch with family members.

Chances are that you don't speak the main language of the country you are going to. If time permits, take language classes online or in person or, better yet, enrol in an immersion program—any of which will make your visit considerably better.

Communicating in another language can be somewhat overwhelming, but I found learning ten words/phrases is a great way to break the ice. Making a small effort to communicate in your host's language goes a long way, and I guarantee that any effort you make will be greeted with delight. And remember to smile!

Web-based translation apps are useful, but you may not have Wi-Fi. Looking at a person's face rather than at your phone establishes a human connection, so start with a few key words/phrases in the local language (see below). You will find lots of opportunity and encouragement to expand your vocabulary during your trip.

....

MY TOP 10 WORDS AND PHRASES
TO LEARN IN THE LOCAL LANGUAGE

Write the translations on a sticky note to carry in your notebook or phone case for quick reference—until you know the words and phrases by heart.

1. Hello
2. How are you?
3. Fine/great
4. Please
5. You're welcome

6. Thank you very much

7. Yes/no

8. Excuse me/sorry

9. Delicious

10. Beautiful

Knowing the word for toilet is very important too!

....

AVOID MAKING HASTY ASSESSMENTS

By now you will have made contact with your NGO, done your research, gotten your travel documents in order, and arranged health care coverage. A word of warning: just because you now have some basic information about where you are going and what your NGO does, you are not an expert! This is only the beginning of your learning journey. It is tempting to jump to conclusions, but don't shortchange yourself. If you think you already know the answers, you will overlook lots of facts that could not only affect your experience but also lead to incorrect judgments.

You are not an expert!

HAVEN'T BEEN THERE BUT KNOW ALL ABOUT IT
DATELINE: 2018 – LONDON. I was at a dinner when one of the guests remarked that "there are no Christians left in Lebanon." I asked him if he had been to Lebanon, and he said although he had not, his great friends were very knowledgeable about the country. By chance, the next day I was flying to Beirut to stay with friends from a Christian family. In fact, there are 17 factions

in Lebanon, 12 of them Christian—so his statement was false. I had no intention of making him look foolish, but I felt it was important to set the record straight. I pointed out that perhaps his friends hadn't visited Lebanon for a while. I had been working in and visiting Lebanon for more than 24 years and knew many Christians living there, and to my knowledge, there was no sign of them leaving en masse.

The gentleman in my London-dinner story isn't alone in making pronouncements with, at best, slivers of information from a singular point of view. When you hear an opinion about the country you are going to visit, remember it is just that: one opinion from one person. Putting too much stock in one person's view can get you into trouble, as countless politicians have discovered. Take all the information you get with a grain of salt and try to determine the sources so you can ascertain a reasonably accurate picture of what to expect.

TRAVEL BY NUMBERS

Use the 24-Hour Clock

To ensure clarity, always use the 24-hour clock (also known as military time), notably when confirming your arrival with your host NGO or hotel.

TIME TRAVEL CONFUSION

DATELINE: FEBRUARY 1995. I flew to Maputo, Mozambique, via Johannesburg, South Africa, from New York. At the time, JFK-JNB was the world's longest non-stop flight, a fact of which I was painfully aware squeezed into my seat for more than 15 hours. Save the Children (SC) had hired me to deliver a microfinance workshop.

The day before my departure, I sent the hotel a fax confirming my arrival date of 10 February with an arrival time of 11 p.m. and received confirmation in Portuguese that a driver would be waiting for me at the airport. After a short connection from Johannesburg, I was relieved that my luggage was already on the baggage carousel. I was exhausted from my long trip and could hardly wait to get a good night's sleep. But when I went through the doors to the arrival hall, there was no driver waiting for me. It was exactly 11 p.m. so I was puzzled and concerned.

Before mobile phones, you had to think on your feet. I had made a note of the hotel's address and recalled that it wasn't too far from the airport. I quickly changed some dollars into the local currency, found a taxi, and got to the hotel without issue.

At the front desk, the man working the late shift looked perplexed when I gave him my name. I asked why no one had met me at the airport. He said that they had expected me at 11 a.m. Then it hit me: a.m. and p.m. are rarely used in many parts of the world, so it was easy to see how the miscommunication came about. There are several flights daily from Johannesburg to Maputo, so they assumed I took an earlier flight and went to stay elsewhere.

Now that the mystery was solved, I asked for my room key. The clerk shifted uncomfortably and said that when they thought I wasn't coming, my room was allocated to another guest. Panic and fatigue set in. I said there must be a room—which there was, but at double the price of the standard room that I had booked. Because this was my error, it meant I would have to pay the difference out of my own pocket. I certainly wasn't going to look for another hotel at this hour, so I provided my credit card and checked into my pricey room. While travelling, I've used the 24-hour clock since!

Get the Scoop on Day-Month-Year

If you are travelling from North America, providing your arrival date can lead to confusion. Around the globe, the majority of countries use the format day, month, year (DD-MM-YYYY). To you, 3/4/2020 might mean March 4, 2020, but it will be interpreted as 3 April 2020 by most people worldwide. Instead of using only numbers, use the abbreviation of the month in letters, along with the day of the week. For example: "I will be arriving on Tuesday, 18 August 2020, at 21:00 at London LHR from Toronto YYZ on AC868."

Interestingly, the approved standard of international date format agreed on in 2015 by the International Organization of Standardization (ISO) is year, month, day (YYYY-MM-DD), which citizens from Canada, China, Korea, Japan, Iran, Hungary, and Lithuania will know. These countries officially adopted the ISO format, while most others stuck to their traditional systems.

Go Metric

The metric system is used to express units of measurement in every country except the United States, Liberia, and Myanmar. If you don't know it, familiarize yourself with it so you know the weight of your luggage in kilograms, the distance to your destination in kilometres, and the temperature you're feeling in Celsius.

COMMUNICATING YOUR TRAVEL ARRANGEMENTS

To avoid potential mix-ups, clearly indicate the following information:

- day, date, and time of arrival
- cities of arrival and departure using the three-letter airport code
- airline and flight number

··

Some Adjustment Needed

Upon arrival, you will discover making calls and charging devices is different from home. Again, it is good to be prepared ahead of time.

- To place a local call when you arrive: If using your mobile, you need to know the code for the country you are in. Press the "+" sign, then the country code, followed by the local area code and phone number. The procedure is slightly different if using a local phone, and your host NGO can explain that.
- To charge your phone: Electrical currents differ from country to country so you most likely will need to bring the correct adapter. A converter, necessary for an appliance, is not required for devices and computers—it is not recommended to bring a hair dryer!

KEY POINTS

1. Ensure information about your host country is from reputable sources.
2. Keep an open mind without forming preconceptions.
3. Make a plan to get visas and health checkups well in advance.
4. Confirm travel arrangements with your host NGO in unambiguous language.

Check out the website *amazingvolunteer.com*

1. Shekinah Rawlings provides useful tips on what to expect when volunteering abroad in the video "Peace Corps | 15 Tips, Hacks and FAQs" (2018).
2. Paul Colto offers advice on how to navigate your new surroundings and how to deal with culture shock in the video "How to Settle Quickly in a New Country—Ten Tips" (2018).
3. Watch Yubing Zhang's TED Talk, "Life Begins at the End of Your Comfort Zone" (2015), on YouTube. Yubing describes exciting moments up ahead once you make the leap to try out new opportunities!

LET'S GET PACKING

He who would travel happily must travel light.
– ANTOINE DE SAINT-EXUPÉRY

TO PACK WELL and appropriately, devote time to planning ahead. If you end up in a remote area, you don't want to be kicking yourself and thinking, "If only I had brought a…" or "If only I hadn't brought all this…"

PERHAPS NOT SUCH A "PERFECT" OUTFIT AFTER ALL
DATELINE: 2007 – MOUNTAINOUS REGION OF A DEVELOPING COUNTRY. Representing a small British NGO, I went to visit three education programs with a small group, including a donor who had brought a heavy suitcase. She was oblivious to the fact that her bag had to be carried up steep unpaved paths to our accommodation. During supper on the first evening, she described the various outfits she had packed, together with matching pairs of sandals. A few glances were exchanged since we were all wondering how she would navigate the footpaths to reach schools in remote areas—and it was the rainy season.

Imagine our hosts' expressions when she appeared all smiles the next morning, after a particularly heavy rainfall, dressed in a pastel outfit and wearing chic sandals. She looked ready to attend a cocktail party, not to trek to the school we were scheduled to visit several kilometres away by foot on a muddy path. It was clear that our travelling companion was going to require a lot of assistance. Without any tread on her sandals, it was hopeless for her to gain traction. Running shoes were located for her to borrow so that she could walk more easily, but within minutes, mud splotches spoiled her outfit. When we arrived at the first school, she was self-conscious about her unattractive footwear and bedraggled outfit, so I doubt she was able to fully enjoy the experience of interacting with the kids.

CHOOSE APPROPRIATE CLOTHING

Having the right attire is absolutely key. When you dress in a practical way, you can focus on learning and being of use rather than fussing about your sartorial choices. Check the location and weather to figure out what you need to wear, making sure it is well-suited for the environment and climate you will be visiting. Your goal is to make a good impression, and you can look tidy and smart without bringing your entire wardrobe. Your trip is not about making fashion statements on your Instagram posts!

Many people in your host community will treat your visit as special, so it is important to take that into consideration—looking like a slob or wearing skimpy items is not cool. In some of the poorest slums, I have seen numerous people dressed in beautifully starched white blouses/shirts and ironed skirts or trousers. People the world over take pride in their appearance, so it can be condescending to "dress down." Dress in such a way that people around you feel comfortable and that you won't be concerned about how you are being perceived by co-workers or the wider community.

It is a sign of respect to dress appropriately, and this will facilitate a smooth interaction with the people you meet. In many countries, tight clothing can be viewed as fashionable. However, in more conservative parts of the world, tight clothing is wholly inappropriate. In many countries and airports, yoga pants, leggings, and sleeveless fitted tops are not considered suitable attire. Loose-fitting tops with trousers and a scarf, to cover up (and protect yourself from the sun), is a good look. For men, showing bare legs is not deemed culturally acceptable in many parts of the world, so save your shorts for the beach. Naturally, if you go to a hotel or a club where there is a pool, it is fine to put on a bathing suit and casual attire once inside the establishment. If you are a runner, find out in advance what sort of clothing would be acceptable in the local community.

Less Is More

Place all the clothes that you think you'd like to take on your bed and then start editing. Use the packing list in Appendix 2 as a guide, and you'll find you require only a fraction of the clothes covering your bed. Mixing and matching is the name of the game—so you don't need a lot of different outfits—practicality and comfort are your goals. Trousers in neutral colours are great for hiding dirt and have the added advantage of not attracting mosquitoes. You can't go wrong with a polo shirt or a loose-fitting blouse that covers your bum, a lightweight longish jacket with pockets, and khaki trousers. Plus, in your host country you will likely be able to buy clothing at reasonable prices, suited to the climate.

Practicality and comfort are your goals.

Make sure that your clothing can be easily washed and doesn't require ironing. Linen has a lovely weight in hot countries, but the fabric wrinkles easily and can look frightful quickly. Lightweight cotton is the best fabric since it breathes and can dry quickly—far superior to many synthetic fabrics that make you feel the heat. And pockets are extremely useful.

RESPECT THE LOCAL DRESS CODE

Ask your host NGO for guidelines about clothing dos and don'ts within the local community. As in most places, urban dwellers are often more cosmopolitan and are accustomed to people dressing in different styles. However, in more remote rural areas where there isn't as much diversity, it is common sense to learn about the basic aspects of your host culture so that you don't unintentionally insult people. Standing out can also put you at risk, and it isn't worth compromising your personal safety to make a fashion statement.

Learn about the basic aspects of your host culture.

There is much discussion nowadays about cultural appropriation in dress and style, so how do you know what is appropriate?

The litmus test is that if the local population is happy for you to wear it, then by all means, enjoy the novelty. For example, wearing a salwar kameez, the dress worn by many women in Bangladesh, is not only practical but also appreciated since you are being respectful by covering most of your body. Putting on jewellery made by Masai in Tanzania or Kenya is likewise a compliment. However, if something is sacred to a culture or is worn to deride an ethnic group in any way, then it is off limits.

One of the highlights of visiting any country is shopping at local markets. Buying locally made clothing and jewellery supports the local economy and stands you in good favour.

Wedding bands are almost universally understood, so wearing a ring on your wedding finger can help ward off unwanted advances. It is a good prop that helps create a barrier to avoid any misunderstandings while retaining professionalism.

MAYBE RECONSIDER THAT MINISKIRT?

DATELINE: MAY 1994 – AMMAN, JORDAN. While working in Beirut, a Lebanese colleague in her 20s and I were asked to travel to Amman for a week-long workshop where I was to be a facilitator. It was the first visit to Jordan for both of us, so we were looking forward to some sightseeing in addition to attending the workshop. My colleague was a fan of miniskirts— fine in Beirut but frowned upon in more conservative Amman.

We checked into our hotel room, and just before leaving, I asked her if she thought wearing such a short skirt might be an issue. She said she was an Arab woman, that it was her right to wear what she pleased and, if people didn't like it, that was their problem and not hers. I didn't want to argue with her on her turf, so we ventured out. We had agreed to have a walk in the downtown area with two male colleagues. They both raised their eyebrows when they saw what my co-worker was wearing, but they also didn't want to broach the obvious issue.

Out on the street, almost immediately men we walked by started making derogatory clicking noises and low whistles, which she merely ignored. This reaction lasted during our entire walk, which made the outing awkward at best, and it could have become more unpleasant. Her stubbornness meant that we were all uncomfortable on what could have been a lovely walk around town. She never admitted her misjudgment, but I noticed she wore jeans from that point on. Lesson learned.

AVOID LUGGING LOTS

Liberate yourself by packing light. Choose one bag to check in and one to carry on. Your checked bag should weigh no more than 22 kilograms and your carry-on no more than 8 kilograms. Anything that isn't absolutely necessary is better left at home. Each should have a baggage tag with your name and contact telephone number—it is not advisable to advertise your home address. Your checked-bag tag should also include the address of your accommodation as well as a local contact number. In the event that your bag does not arrive when you do, it can be delivered to your local address. And just in case that might happen, it is always a good idea to review all that you are taking with you and make sure the absolute necessities are in your carry-on, including a change of clothes and a small toiletry kit with any essential medicines.

Choose one bag to check in and one to carry on.

Make sure you can easily carry all of your luggage so you don't burden yourself or others with a lot of unnecessary stuff. Often there aren't paved roads on which to wheel a roller bag, so be prepared to carry your bag if necessary. You don't want to come across as a high-maintenance visitor with excess baggage right from the start.

Make sure you can easily carry all of your luggage.

Think Smart About What You Carry On

Your carry-on bag should meet the standard size for all airlines and weigh 8 kilograms or less. Use it much like a Russian nesting doll set by selecting a smaller lightweight backpack that easily fits inside it—a clever trick if you are limited to only one piece of carry-on. You can stow your carry-on in the overhead compartment, and keep your backpack of in-flight essentials under the seat in front of you.

In addition, I advise getting a crossbody bag to safeguard all your essentials (wallet, passport, phone, contact sheet) and to keep it on wherever you go.

THE ESSENTIALS: PASSPORT, MONEY, AND PHONE

Two cardinal rules of travel: 1) never be parted from your passport and 2) keep your cash with you at all times. Keep your passport and cash in a crossbody bag, a money belt, or an inside pocket of a jacket that goes with you everywhere. Storing them in the outside pocket of your backpack is asking for trouble. Once you are familiar with your lodgings, there may be someplace safe to keep valuables, or often you can lock away your passport and wallet in your host NGO's safe.

Ask your local contact in advance if and where you can find an ATM at your destination. You can try using your debit card to get local cash from an ATM upon arrival, but don't be dismayed if it doesn't work or if there isn't one. You can usually find an ATM in the lobby of an international hotel. Bear in mind that there will be service charges with each withdrawal. If given an option, don't take the foreign exchange rate offered by the ATM—it is a rip-off!

Inform your bank and credit card company before travelling that you will be accessing your account and using your card overseas. That way neither will be blocked for suspicious activity.

US dollars are still widely used in many countries where banks aren't numerous. Almost anywhere in the world, it is advisable to bring US dollars, which are accepted at any foreign exchange kiosk, commonly referred to as a bureau de change. Bring $1, $5, $10, $20, $50, and $100 denominations. If you aren't able to change money into the local currency upon arrival, you can always give someone a few US dollars for a tip. You get a better exchange rate with large bills ($50 and $100 denominations) and often new bills only are accepted (the concern is that older notes could be counterfeit). Money changers usually don't like dirty bills, so try to bring currency that is in a decent condition (no marks, writing, or rips).

It is advisable to bring US dollars.

However, be warned that in many rural areas changing US dollars can be tricky, so make sure you have a sufficient amount of local currency before you leave the capital. If there is no ATM at the airport, you can change US$100 at the airport's bureau de change. In some countries, locals can't use US dollars, so first check which is the preferred hard currency (most often USD or Euros). Also, it is worth noting that credit cards are not usually accepted in places where there isn't much tourism.

Even if you can get a better rate of exchange outside the airport, the ease and convenience of having some local currency in your pocket as soon as you arrive is a good idea. It makes it easy to tip and pay for taxis, water, or snacks.

The third essential, your phone, is a lifeline: the holder of so much information. Because you never know when your phone might die, break, or be stolen, it's important to have a notebook as backup. Record contact names, phone numbers, your itinerary, and any other key information in it. Also, carry an In Case of Emergency (ICE) card in your phone case with details (name, phone number, e-mail address) of whom to contact in your host country as well as in your home country. Finally, investigate your phone plan well in advance of your departure.

STRIPPING FOR MONEY

DATELINE: DECEMBER 2007 – ABUJA, NIGERIA. I took a short trip to Nigeria with two members from my travel club whom I'd met only briefly. We arrived in the capital Abuja, where I had booked a driver to take us north to Kano. I wanted to change some dollars into the local currency at the airport, but one of my travel companions, a retired banker, was adamant that we would get a much better deal elsewhere. He insisted that we wait until we found a bureau de change en route. I pointed out that we weren't going to exchange a large amount of money, but he felt—out of principle—that we could get a better rate. I wanted to start the trip on a good note so agreed.

Within the hour, we stopped at a "recommended" money changer, which the driver assured us would give us a preferential rate. Our banker travelling companion took charge by saying that we had a lot of money to exchange, so we wanted the best rate for our dollars. The money changers asked how much we wanted to exchange; in a low voice, the banker said, "US$300." They smiled, stated their rate, and then the banker looked pleased, feeling that he had secured a good deal.

I produced my US$100 bill from my bag as did our other travel mate. The banker went to retrieve his money, which he had securely hidden underneath his clothing. He proceeded to untuck his shirt and then his undershirt to get at his money belt, only to find that it was entangled in the belt holding up his trousers. It was an amusing, albeit cringeworthy, sight watching this seasoned traveller struggle to reach a US$100 bill. In a rather dishevelled state, with all of us trying not to look at him, he handed over his bank note. One of the money changers then produced a huge wad of US dollars, casually added our pittance of a contribution, and peeled off the local currency equivalent.

It was evident that the official rate at the airport would have been to our advantage, but to keep the peace, we all went along with the pretense that we had done very well.

KEY POINTS

1. Take time to pack strategically—travelling light is liberating.
2. Be respectful by wearing appropriate clothing.
3. Take cash in US dollars.

Check out the website *amazingvolunteer.com*

1. Take a look at the "Essential Packing List" (also in Appendix 2) and print a copy.
2. Watch the video "Volunteer Abroad: How to Pack Like a Pro" (International Volunteer HQ, 2016).
3. Watch the 30-second video "What to Wear in Southeast Asia" (Ashley Nelson, 2016).

Part 3

ADAPTING TO A
NEW ENVIRONMENT

PRACTICALITIES OF YOUR ARRIVAL

Do the best you can do until you know better.
Then when you know better, do better.
– MAYA ANGELOU

NO DOUBT AFTER the buildup and anticipation of your voyage, it is really exciting to finally get to your destination. All your well-laid plans can now come to fruition. You have left behind your somewhat predictable day-to-day life for an adventure where the future is unknown. Make sure you kick things off well by knowing what to do when you arrive, but don't worry when not all goes according to plan.

OUT OF YOUR COMFORT ZONE

If this is your first visit to a developing country, you will probably find it quite jarring.

Everything will seem relatively standard when you disembark from the plane and get to the baggage carousel. Things will look somewhat familiar, albeit the signage will be in a different language. The shock comes when you exit the airport and your senses go into overdrive. Even though I had been travelling in Southeast Asia, the first time I flew into Delhi in June 1986, I wasn't prepared for the wall of heat that hit me as I left the airport terminal at 3 a.m.! Amid all the intoxicating smells, it was also bewildering to see masses of people lined up waiting for relatives. I literally felt as though I had stepped into another world. While it was thrilling, I felt a bit anxious as I had no idea what to expect. There is nothing to fear—take a deep breath and absorb your new environment.

REALITY BITES

NINE DAYS AFTER ARRIVING IN BANGLADESH
FAX TO: Elizabeth Gibson, Toronto, Canada
FROM: Susan Gibson, Dhaka, Bangladesh
DATE: 9 April 1992

Dear Mum,

I'm fine and adjusting well to life in Dhaka. I hope you receive this fax without any problems. It is impossible to call collect from Bangladesh and I don't have access to a phone.

Saturday is moving day to our apartment. Our Bangladeshi classmate has been so helpful in getting us set up. We had a look at it today and it will be fine—there are two very basic washrooms with showers. It is unfurnished, so we will buy mattresses from the market and pick up a few pieces of furniture. We bought ceiling fans in Thailand and they are being installed tomorrow. Without them, sleep would be rather elusive. It has been 38C every day, with humidity at 65% and this is just the beginning of spring!

We have spent the week getting to know Dhaka and have started our Bangla lessons. Our teacher is very good—our lessons are two and a half hours every day, five days a week. I'm coming along with the Sanskrit numbers but have not attempted the alphabet yet (60 letters!!). People are very encouraging when I say a few words in Bangla, so I hope I'll be able to get by with the basics in seven weeks.

I had my second meeting at Grameen Bank today and I'm excited about my future involvement there. It turns out they need to train some of their senior staff in English conversation—I'm glad I can be of use. I'll also see how they set up microlending units. I'll write more soon. Love, Susie

That's what I wrote to my mum. However, my first diary entry after arriving in Bangladesh shows life was rather more dramatic behind the scenes!

TWO DAYS AFTER ARRIVING IN BANGLADESH

DIARY ENTRY: 2 APRIL 1992 – DHAKA, BANGLADESH. I was so happy when we first arrived and then things quickly deteriorated. I'm just relieved that I am alive after yesterday. I must have picked up giardia [a nasty parasite] in Thailand and became very ill. I was up all night when we arrived and felt miserable the following day. I ate breakfast this morning and finally feel much better. I barely made it to our first Bangla lesson. Then we hung out at the American Club for the better part of the afternoon. We met the usual expats—a know-it-all who loved a new audience and a couple of navy personnel.

Yesterday, I had visions of having to book my flight home, but everything has improved a hundred-fold today. One flatmate got out his "Where There Is No Doctor" [standard issue for Peace Corps volunteers], and he took great pleasure in reading out all the disgusting symptoms for giardia, which is how we figured out what I had.

At one point yesterday, I had a dizzy spell and grabbed the wardrobe in the room I was sharing with my female flatmate, and the bottle of gin we bought at duty free crashed on the floor. I can't imagine what the staff in the guesthouse think—booze on the carpet, the four of us all in and out of each other's rooms, and me in bed all day—not a good first impression for our Muslim hosts.

SET UP AN EMERGENCY CONTACT

Although I had a bit of a rough time during my first couple of days, it was immeasurably better not to share the details of what was going on with my mother. She would have been concerned and wanted to help. The three classmates with whom I went to Bangladesh and our classmate from Dhaka were all people I could rely on to get the assistance I needed. Pointlessly worrying my mother who was 12,500 kilometres away would not have confirmed which parasite I had contracted.

Upon arrival, it's important to establish some sort of safety net—people you can call in an emergency and who can check on you—be it the group members you are travelling with or a local contact person at your host NGO. Be sure to add the local telephone contact information on your phone and jot it down in your notebook so if you run into trouble, you can easily text/call someone. Most issues, like getting ill, although unpleasant, are easily addressed. Sometimes the biggest challenge is locating a decent bathroom when you are not well—and that too is not something your mother can help you with.

Establish some sort of safety net—
people you can call in an emergency.

ADOPT A POSITIVE OUTLOOK AND AN OPEN MIND

It is a good idea to manage your expectations. Putting yourself in a new environment will challenge you mentally, physically, and emotionally—the highs are really high and the lows are very low. You will be tested by a range of issues that you haven't had to face back home, including questionable modes of local transportation, intense heat, connectivity problems, power cuts, health concerns, bizarre insects, personality clashes, the availability of flush toilets, and simply not finding a place to feel comfortable.

You will discover a lot about yourself and perhaps learn more about what motivates you and what you fundamentally value. There will be some bumps along the way, but the experiences often lead to a broadening of your horizons.

Manage your expectations.

Whatever the reality in your new environment, you can bet it will be very different from your situation back home. Don't be quick to judge, criticize, or make comparisons: "That's not how we do it where I come from." No kidding. Avoid the us-versus-them mentality because it is condescending. Instead, focus on the similarities you share rather than dwelling on differences. Remember, unless you have something nice to say, be quiet and see what you can learn.

Don't be quick to judge, criticize, or make comparisons.

The challenge that you are setting for yourself is meant to push you. The rewards of the experience won't magically materialize without overcoming some hurdles. Have patience and accept that the pace of life won't be what you are accustomed to. Wishing things to happen quickly will lead to disappointment.

Accept that you can only do so much to direct outcomes. Although things won't often go smoothly, let go of being in control: accept the process and you will be much happier. You might be surprised that with options previously not considered, you find yourself open to being more creative in your approach—take a chance to see what happens when you choose a new path. Coming from a perspective where "time is money" and value is placed on getting things done as efficiently as possible, annoyances can materialize quickly.

Let go of being in control.

Given that you are a volunteer, take a step back, listen, watch, and learn. If you are approaching the experience on a transactional basis, then I'm afraid you will be disappointed. A volunteer is someone who willingly performs a service without pay and does so without expecting anything in return. Eighty per cent of your satisfaction as a volunteer will depend on how you manage the forks in the road, so work on handling challenges with grace and humility. By taking risks, you *will* make mistakes—what is important is what you learn from the experience: choose courage over comfort.

Listen, watch, and learn.

ARRIVAL CHECKLIST

Common sense is the best tool in your toolbox. You are treading on new terrain, so don't do anything foolish that could get you into trouble. You are a guest in another country, and you have willingly gone to visit. Therefore, you must respect the local laws and the people living there.

The following are the main issues to consider as soon as you land.

1. Practice Good Hygiene Habits

Given the impact of COVID-19 worldwide, make sure you wear your face mask when around others and ensure you carry hand sanitizer at all times. In developing countries, access to running water is an issue and hand sanitizer is expensive for many people to buy. Other WHO guidelines include:

- Don't shake hands or hug anyone.

- Avoid touching your face with unclean hands.
- Wash your hands with soap and water for 20 seconds frequently (or use hand sanitizer).
- Sneeze and cough into the crook of your arm.
- As much as possible, try to maintain a physical distance from people and meet out of doors or in well-ventilated indoor areas.

2. Register with Your Country's Embassy or High Commission

Make it a priority to provide a contact number and details of your whereabouts to your country's government representative so they can help if you need assistance. Sign up for country alerts to keep informed of changing circumstances in your host country.

3. Familiarize Yourself with Local Laws

Know what they are and respect them, especially pertaining to drugs, medicines, and alcohol. Trafficking bears the death penalty in many countries. The vast majority of problems that embassy personnel have to contend with are visitors getting into trouble with alcohol or drugs.

4. Be Respectful of the Local Culture

Read up on the culture and what religions are practiced—adhere to cultural etiquette. You've packed appropriate clothes, so now be sure to wear them. "When in Rome, do as the Romans do." Always have a long scarf in your bag in case you need to cover up.

5. Exercise Caution with Social Media

•

Consider how your posts might affect others. Even though you may have been updating your Instagram story daily at home, it might be a good time to take a break. Before you post *anything*, check with your host NGO about a code of conduct for sharing photos. Promoting the NGO's work on social media may be helpful, but it is extremely important to respect their boundaries and guidelines. *Do not* post pictures of locals without their permission, especially children—you might be putting them at risk. Practice self-censorship—issues can arise with oversharing. Ideally, take your first couple of days to absorb what you are experiencing without documenting it. You might feel liberated!

6. Keep in Touch with Family and Friends

•

Be prepared to contend with limited access to Wi-Fi. Make sure that your family members know you have arrived safely and when you settle in, figure out the best way to communicate on a regular basis. WhatsApp is commonly used, so getting a local SIM card might be the most economical way to use your phone, depending on your location. Get advice from your colleagues about the best way to keep in touch locally to prevent roaming charges, which add up quickly. However, in order for you to make the most of your experience, it is not necessary to provide a running commentary of your every move. In fact, too much contact with loved ones back home may stop you from opening yourself up to new friends and colleagues. At times, you will likely be homesick and feel like you are missing out on events at home. Taking a break from social media platforms helps you focus on being present in your new environment. You can't successfully be in two places at once. New friends will appreciate you paying attention to them, not to someone's party several thousand kilometres away.

🍁 🍁 🍁

From the moment you arrive and almost without fail, people will ask you where you are from before they ask your name. Like it or not, that makes you an unofficial ambassador of your country, so make your compatriots proud. Be aware of your surroundings and get guidance from knowledgeable local people. It takes lots of energy to be a good listener but the information you will receive will help you adapt. Having a successful start boils down to being respectful in your host country and using common sense.

THAT'S SOBERING

Three vignettes come to mind that highlight the differences of a life lived in safety and privilege compared to one where people face danger and survive in poverty.

HOPES AND DREAMS

DATELINE: MARCH 1992 – PHANAT NIKHOM REFUGEE CAMP, THAILAND. On my way to start my internship in Bangladesh, my classmates and I stopped off in Thailand for two weeks. We went to visit a refugee camp where one flatmate had done his Peace Corps stint a few years earlier. The head teacher welcomed short-term volunteers to teach English classes for refugees who were waiting to be approved for refugee status in the US, Canada, or Australia—the wait was long and not successful for most.

We had a lesson plan to follow and the topic for the day was goals and aspirations. A suggested question was to ask what people wished for in the future. A young man from the persecuted Hmong hill tribe put up his hand and answered: "I just want to be a citizen of any country."

DATELINE: MARCH 1995 – BRAC CENTRE FOR DEVELOPMENT MANAGEMENT (CDM), RAJENDRAPUR, BANGLADESH. Three years after my internship at Grameen Bank, I organized a microcredit management program for Women's World Banking (WWB) network affiliates from several African countries.

I was delighted to have the opportunity to take the participants to a village to show them Grameen Bank in action. Grameen borrowers were accustomed to having Bangladeshi visitors but they had never seen Africans, so there was a great deal of curiosity. After a group meeting, with 40 female borrowers in attendance, we had the chance to ask questions. Questions such as "What do you do with your loan proceeds?" and "What challenges do you have with your income-generating activity?" were standard, but we were also encouraged to ask borrowers what their hopes were.

I asked a woman in the front row what her dream was, to which she replied, "I want to be able to write my name."

DATELINE: NOVEMBER 2012 – BUKAVU, LAKE KIVU, DEMOCRATIC REPUBLIC OF THE CONGO (DRC). I was on a donor trip to visit a group of NGOs that receive grants from the Fund for

Global Human Rights (FGHR). One of the recipient NGOs was Le Bureau pour le Volontariat au service de l'Enfance et de la Santé (BVES), whose mission was to rehabilitate child soldiers. While walking around the compound for the rescued girls (the boys were at a different location), we were welcomed by about 200 girls who were all being housed, getting educated, and learning skills to earn an income.

We stopped by the area where approximately 100 babies were being cared for so that their mothers—girls themselves under the age of 18—could go to school on the compound. It was inconceivable to comprehend that almost every girl there had been raped multiple times, and in addition to the trauma they had experienced, they now had babies to raise.

One girl was asked what she needed, and she replied, "I need a birth certificate for my baby, but the Congolese government won't recognize my baby because I was raped by a Ugandan soldier."

Those three exchanges in Thailand, Bangladesh, and the DRC are as clear to me now as they were when they took place decades ago. As someone who never had to worry about the safety of my neighbourhood nor wonder if my parents could afford to send me to school or protect me from people who commit atrocities—I had never considered how these fundamental concerns plague many of the world's poorest populations.

I have to admit that on these occasions I was on the verge of tears but managed to maintain my composure. It is crucial not to look down on anyone: no one wants your pity. You don't want to give anyone the impression that their situation is hopeless. Be tactful and empathetic—it is better to say, "I'm very sorry this has happened to you." You may have a strong, visceral reaction but always keep in mind that you are a guest and are not there to judge, only to observe. It is not all about you! You will have to find a way to process information that you are confronted with but do it in a way that, first and foremost, takes into consideration people's feelings. And don't think for a moment you can understand what it's really like for people living in difficult circumstances.

Be tactful and empathetic.

"SKIP BREAKFAST AND SUFFER WITH THE PEOPLE"

DIARY ENTRY: 30 APRIL 1991 – PORT-AU-PRINCE, HAITI. A group of American missionaries arrived at the guesthouse today. During their briefing, the leader informed them they were not going to eat breakfast today so they could know what it's like to be hungry and suffer with the Haitian people. What nonsense— and how insulting! Choosing not to eat is entirely different from not having food to eat. It's patronizing to think that you can understand what it's like to be hungry purely by skipping a meal.

Encountering the shock and scale of poverty that is prevalent in developing countries where many NGOs operate is jarring. It is impossible to imagine how an incalculable number of people can exist in slums or in makeshift structures on the pavement. It isn't a fair world, and it *should* be upsetting to witness people suffering and surviving in conditions that are beyond comprehension. Hence the existence of hundreds of thousands of NGOs around the world to address the injustices and challenges that hundreds of millions of people are forced to endure.

It should *be upsetting to witness people suffering.*

EMBRACE WHERE YOU ARE

DIARY ENTRY: 6 APRIL 1992 – DHAKA, BANGLADESH. We went for a walk by the slums nearby our apartment where we were invited into two very modest homes. I can't imagine inviting a stranger passing by into our house back home. The people were hospitable and were pleased that we'd sit with them. The children were adorable and curious. It isn't fair that they live in such dilapidated housing when I have so much. I don't want to think about it too much because it makes me feel uncomfortable.

The three of us then ended up at a small fairground. We attracted crowds everywhere we walked—people gawked at us and many spoke to us. We tested out the Ferris wheel—the safety measures were lax, putting it mildly.

Bangla (or Bengali as the Brits call the language) is going to be a challenge but possible. Because of Eid al Adha (the holiday at the end of Ramadan), it has been very quiet. It has given us time to adjust to Dhaka without traffic and get familiar with our neighbourhood near the parliament buildings and the Arong store where visitors buy handicrafts.

When we all start our internships, our time will be completely taken up with our work and Bangla lessons. We hired Ashi, a woman who will come in to do the cooking. There are no appliances in the kitchen! It is a room with a sink and no counter, and the little gas cooker we bought sits on the floor. We smile a lot at each other because it is hard to communicate, but that will improve as our Bangla progresses. It is convenient and necessary to have someone cook and wash for us—going out to buy food daily at the market, preparing meals, and doing laundry without modern appliances would consume an entire day.

DIARY ENTRY: 8 APRIL 1992, 9:30 P.M. – DHAKA, BANGLADESH.
I'm feeling much more settled now. At Grameen Bank, it was decided that my teaching English conversation to senior staff would be helpful. For me to understand how the Grameen model works, I'm being sent out to spend a week or so in the countryside to visit branches to learn how microlending groups are established. Doing some teaching and going on field trips to do research is a good combination.

Our apartment looks adequate although it will be sparsely furnished. We have mattresses on the bedroom floors with a bamboo shelving unit each and mats to sit on in the living room. I'll be happy to move in over the weekend.

ABSORBING CULTURE SHOCK

Culture shock is completely normal and unavoidable—everyone experiences it in varying degrees. There is a model to help you understand what you go through when you enter a new culture. Understanding culture shock will help you adapt. A brief summary is as follows:

1. Honeymoon phase:
"This was a great decision to come!"

The first stage is when you first arrive and find everything exciting. Generally, you are feeling overwhelmingly positive. This is when you pat yourself on the back.

2. Frustration phase: "What in the world was I thinking?!"

•

The second phase can kick in anywhere from a day to several weeks after you arrive, depending on how smoothly things go for you. It is usually triggered when you face some sort of difficulty, and you will feel homesick.

3. Adjustment phase: "I'm here and I have to make the best of it."

•

At this point, your irritations become more subdued as you begin to feel more familiar and somewhat comfortable with the culture, people, food, and language in your new environment. With support from your local friends and community, you are able to "go with the flow."

4. Acceptance phase: "There are positive and negative aspects about any place."

•

You now enjoy the best of what you are exposed to and avoid the worst. You come to the realization that there is no perfect place. While you're away, you'll likely wish for home and then when you get home, you'll idealize the place you left.

Understanding culture shock will help you adapt.

🍁 🍁 🍁

While living in Dhaka, I disliked being followed and having every move scrutinized. It was easy to feel annoyed, but I worked at accepting the new dynamic. I quickly realized that I wasn't going to be able to change how the local population reacted to my presence, so I would have to adjust my attitude. Although prying eyes were ever-present, I reminded myself that I, being a white woman from Canada, was in fact a curiosity and that people were naturally interested in why I was in their country. It was all part of the experience.

SHOCK REMEDY

An old friend who has done six tours with the US Department of State and three with the military offers the following advice:

> When arriving in a new country, almost daily, I find I need to remind myself that feelings of being overwhelmed, frustrated, and excited are perfectly normal and are to be expected. A good night's sleep, talking to someone or writing in a journal, and a cup of tea can be just what the doctor ordered to calm me and change my mood.

EVEN WITH EXPERIENCE, IT IS EASY TO STUMBLE

DATELINE: JANUARY 1994 – BEIRUT, LEBANON. At the age of 32, I took my first trip to the Middle East. Despite having volunteered and worked in Haiti, Bangladesh, Guyana, and southern Africa, going to a country that I hadn't visited before—and one that was emerging from civil war—was an interesting prospect. I had signed a two-week contract with SC to organize a microfinance workshop for local staff in Beirut. The SC office had been delivering food aid during Lebanon's seventeen-year-long civil war, but now that the fighting had stopped, there was a shift in programming to help people devastated by the conflict rebuild their lives.

Having packed mostly lightweight clothing—thinking it would be mild in the Mediterranean—I landed in Beirut and was taken aback to find that it was damp and cold. Clearly, my spring wardrobe wasn't going to get much use.

SC had sent a driver to collect me. There were soldiers everywhere and numerous roadblocks, which was unnerving. The driver dropped me off at the Mayflower Hotel and told me he would be back to pick me up in the morning. My room was dreary but sufficient, however there were no dining facilities. Later that evening, I was hungry so I asked at reception where I could find a restaurant. Communication was limited, but I got vague directions to a burger place called Uncle Sam's.

Evidence of the war was everywhere. On the streets, there were destroyed and crumbling buildings, damaged cars left haphazardly, and masses of hanging electrical wires. It was already dark and with no street lights, I couldn't see much. Feeling uncertain but determined, I made my way along the uneven road where all the store fronts were boarded up. Hamra, the neighbourhood in which I found myself, was known for its warren of small winding, unsigned streets. My trip to Beirut was years before Google Maps or GPS so it wasn't surprising that I was soon lost. And now, I had no clue which way to go or how to get back to the hotel. Spotting a group of soldiers in a sandbag dugout up ahead, I approached them to ask for directions. It was then that I realized I had no idea if I was in East or West Beirut. I knew that one side of the city was predominantly Christian and the other Muslim, but I didn't know which was which. Aside from the infamous war images of Beirut on television, my knowledge of the fighting along the Green Line that divided the city was pitifully deficient.

My first instinct as I got close to the soldiers was to use the Muslim greeting "as-Salaam Alaikum" (peace be upon you), but what if they were Christians who might find my greeting provocative? Who knows why I didn't just say "hello"—I guess my nerves got the better of me. Out of nowhere, I blurted out, "Shalom." Of all the things to say, this was the one thing that I shouldn't have! Lebanon was at war with Israel so a greeting in Hebrew was perhaps the worst option. The soldiers just stared at me, so I switched to French and asked where Uncle Sam's restaurant was. Again, I was met with blank faces. Great—now they think I am an American Zionist (and Americans weren't permitted to be in Lebanon at that time). Finally, I tried English and said, "It's okay, I'll just head off this way." With that, I turned and walked with purpose down the road, half expecting to get shot for my disastrous efforts, but nothing happened.

After a few minutes of walking with my heart in my mouth, I was relieved to come across a little restaurant where the elderly proprietor invited me to sit down and eat. Feeling apprehensive, I asked him if he could simply direct me to Uncle Sam's. Speaking only a bit of English, he insisted on driving me and with no other obvious alternative, I accepted. Within minutes, he dropped me off at Uncle Sam's where I got a burger. Afterwards, a waiter kindly walked me back to my hotel. I later learned that I was staying near the American University of Beirut on Bliss Street— needless to say, I was unaware that this was the street that was infamous for hostage taking during the civil war.

The next morning at the SC office, I had my introductory meeting with the country director. He apologized for not meeting me for dinner to give me a customary briefing session and asked how I had fared the night before. Without thinking, I related the entire experience, and he exclaimed, "What kind of bloody liability have they sent me?!" He was incredulous but felt responsible that I had been left to my own devices to wander around looking for dinner. After a rocky start, we quickly got on well and ended up having dinner most nights together. We remained friends for many years to come.

Packing unsuitable attire was a novice mistake, but inadvertently saying the wrong thing to soldiers and taking a lift from a stranger could have put me in serious danger. Who knows what the soldiers made of me! It turned out they were Syrian, the occupying force in those days. They likely thought I was odd, but with hostilities running high, I could have been perceived as a threat. The most important lesson from my first night out in Beirut was that you should always make sure you have someone local show you the ropes when you arrive in an unfamiliar place. I was lucky that the old restaurateur was happy to go out of his way to help a visitor. Most people are genuinely decent and willing to offer assistance, regardless of where you are in the world, but you have to use common sense.

A CANADIAN METAPHOR: POWER BOAT VS. CANOE

I love spending time in nature paddling a canoe and thought of a comparison to a power boat that might be helpful when thinking about adapting in a new environment.

Power boats are fast, noisy, aggressive, and cover lots of territory. Going full steam ahead with enthusiasm when setting out on an adventure can be appealing. However, there can be unmarked rocks under the surface, unseen without the benefit of experience, a guide, and a comprehensive map. The wake behind a power boat can do damage that you might not consider. Think of yourself as a canoe when you come to a new environment. Canoes are silent and can easily change course when encountering a rock or getting into the weeds. Canoes don't generate waves and therefore don't create negative effects.

KEY POINTS

1. All your preparations might not be sufficient, but that's okay. Take a deep breath.
2. Create a checklist for what you need to do upon arrival.
3. Culture shock is unavoidable but knowing the stages will help you adjust.

Check out the website *amazingvolunteer.com*

1. Watch the video "TV2: All That We Share," which demonstrates similarities among people from all walks of life (TV2 Danmark, 2017).
2. Take a look at the video "We Survived Culture Shock: Here's How You Can Too" (GoAbroad.com, 2017).

THE NECESSITIES: TOILETS, WATER, FOOD, AND MORE

There are no foreign lands.
It is the traveller only who is foreign.
– ROBERT LOUIS STEVENSON

THERE WILL BE some immediate needs that you will want to address at the beginning of your stay. Among the most important are finding a lavatory, locating safe drinking water, and figuring out your meals.

STRAIGHTFORWARD TOILET TALK

When you arrive at your destination, flush toilets will not always be easy to locate. In wealthier countries, euphemisms such as "washroom," "restroom," or "loo" are used, but what we are all in search of is a toilet and sink. If this is the first time you are venturing further afield, brace yourself: the facilities may not be what you are accustomed to.

In developing countries, finding a place to "go" when mother nature calls can become a preoccupation. You need to adapt to how people locally use outhouses, pit latrines, squat toilets, and drop holes—all are places where you can relieve yourself but take some getting used to if you have only used flush toilets. You might want to be prepared by bringing your own toilet paper, hand sanitizer, and wipes to complete your "washroom" experience.

News alert: the majority of people in the world do not use toilet paper. At a typical squat toilet, you will find a bucket of water on the side. You have to use your left hand to rinse off your behind and then wash your hand. If you are not in the know about toilet practices in developing countries you might have a hard time getting your head around coming into direct contact with your bottom. If the thought of this isn't for you, simply bring your own supply of toilet paper and then dispose of it— in a basket, if available, or in a small plastic bag that you carry with you for just this purpose. Do not put toilet paper in a squat toilet since it will cause clogging.

For men, finding a place to pee isn't much of an issue. One of my flatmates in Dhaka used to say, "The world is your toilet when you're a man." This is not the case for women, where some privacy is required—planning in advance is highly recommended. When travelling overseas, whenever I came across an operational, clean flush toilet—at a rest stop on a highway, for instance—I would use the toilet, regardless of whether I needed it. And I would remember its location for the future.

When you are travelling to places where the infrastructure can be somewhat lacking, find out in advance what to expect about sanitation essentials or you might be in for a rude awakening.

Find out in advance what to
expect about sanitation essentials.

TOP PRIORITY: POTABLE WATER

Above all, to remain in good health, you need to identify where you are going to get your ongoing supply of safe drinking water. When it is hot, dehydration is a risk—you need to drink at least twice as much as you normally do in a cooler climate.

With few exceptions, you cannot drink tap water in developing countries, so bottled or purified water is a must. Ideally, find a clean source of drinking water at your accommodation, where you can continually top up your water bottle. You can buy plastic bottles of water in almost all market areas, just make sure the safety seal is intact. Using your own water bottle will address the issue of single-use plastic bottles. If potable water is hard to come by, buy a coconut, where available, and drink the coconut water to quench your thirst safely.

Bottled or purified water is a must.

Water-borne illnesses are common and, in the case of cholera, can be lethal, so it is critical to always consider the source of your drinking water. Diarrhea is a very common condition; by drinking clean water and practicing good hygiene, you can avoid getting the runs.

If you have a place to boil water, you can set up a simple system of boiling water vigorously for five minutes and then letting it sit to cool down. If you are fortunate to have access to a refrigerator, always keep a jug filled with purified water. You can also bring a water bottle that has an inbuilt purifier, use a SteriPen, or use chlorine or iodine to make safe drinking water, but the taste leaves a lot to be desired.

WATER WATCH

It only takes a drop of contaminated water to make you ill, so you have to be vigilant. For example:

- Be careful with ice cubes. Do not consume them unless you are confident that they are made from purified water, as at an international hotel.
- Beware of fruit without a skin, salad, and ice cream. Unless you are certain that they come from a reliable source, it is better to skip eating these.
- When brushing your teeth, do not rinse your mouth with anything but purified water. If you are short on safe drinking water, you can always use Coke, which is available almost everywhere—not ideal but it won't make you sick.

FOOD, GLORIOUS FOOD

Part of the joy of travelling is sampling local dishes and being able to share a meal with your hosts. You will undoubtedly be offered food on many occasions, and it can be a truly bonding experience. Accepting hospitality is an important social interaction, not only to be polite but also as a matter of diplomacy. People with limited resources go to great lengths to make you feel welcome, so rejecting their hospitality is considered rude and unkind.

I am envious of people who are keen to eat anything and everything. Tasting new dishes has always been a challenge for me since I don't have adventurous taste buds and spiciness doesn't agree with me. I cope by finding one palatable-to-me thing on the table or on the menu and eat it with gusto: "This rice is the best I have ever had!" It is my issue and I never want any fuss to be made. I often poke fun at myself if people inquire about my smaller portions. The attention should always be on the kindness of your hosts and not on your needs. If you do have dietary requirements, it is best to make a plan in advance of how you are going to deal with social situations.

FOODS DO NOT APPEAL TO ALL EQUALLY

DATELINE: DECEMBER 1994 – EASTERN TRANSVAAL, REPUBLIC OF SOUTH AFRICA (RSA). I organized a credit management workshop for 20 participants for WWB affiliates from several African countries and India. It was an exhilarating time to be in RSA: people were full of hope with apartheid being dismantled. It was the first international trip for the majority of the participants, who never would have dreamt of travelling to the birthplace of Nelson Mandela.

For the workshop venue, the local affiliate had secured a good deal at a picturesque safari lodge, a two-hour drive east of the Johannesburg airport. We had ample space for our ten-day workshop and stylish huts for accommodation.

I arrived a day early with my colleague to make sure everything was in good order. The lodge had catered to Europeans, so the meals served appealed to me. On the day everyone arrived, a

Zulu chef cooked the kick-off dinner with local flair. Everyone was thrilled and ate well.

The following day when I was checking in with everyone, several people said they didn't feel well. It turned out that the breakfast buffet didn't offer food that was familiar to them—most were missing cassava, a staple in their diet. I went to see the owner of the lodge to discuss adding food items that would appeal to our participants. He was accustomed to serving Europeans and hadn't considered food preferences for African guests. I suggested that we hire the Zulu chef for the ten days left in our stay, which he reluctantly agreed to do. The energy of the workshop changed markedly now that everyone had the sustenance they needed to concentrate on the task at hand.

In more remote areas in developing countries, volunteers can experience meal monotony, eating the same food day in day out. The important thing is to find easily accessible foods you can eat so that you get the proper nutrition you need to stay feeling well. Manage your expectations since food variety is likely to be limited. Being a vegetarian/vegan can be tricky in some countries, so check ahead that you will be able to get the food you need. Consider bringing multivitamins to make up for any deficiencies in your diet.

Food variety is likely to be limited.

Once you get your bearings and you know what foods are readily available, you can request them, within reason. Ask your hosts about food that is sold locally. For a change, if you get a chance to go to a market area, there are often stalls selling street food to take away. Generally speaking, there is little risk in picking up hot, freshly cooked food, but do watch out for food that has been sitting out since flies will certainly be attracted to it.

Meals are meant to be shared. Sitting down to a meal is a good way to get to know the locals as well as your fellow volunteers. When I was in Haiti on my first overseas volunteer stint, I couldn't figure out why the missionaries and volunteers didn't have meals with the Haitians. The reply was that the volunteers didn't socialize with the locals: they were there to serve them. What a missed opportunity—that made the gap between the groups wider. Eating together is a chance to build strong teams by connecting with people on a personal level, apart from a work environment. Some of my happiest memories of working in Beirut were having lunch every day around a big table, where we all congregated to take a break together and to share food and stories.

Eating together is a chance to build strong teams.

EVERYONE NEEDS THEIR COMFORT FOOD

DATELINE: JUNE 1995 – AMMAN, JORDAN. I was retained by SC to do a workshop for their credit officers. Upon arrival, I was pleased to find out that the director had contracted a Grameen Bank branch manager to come from Bangladesh to improve the microcredit operations.

It was the first international travel experience for the Grameen Bank staff member. He was a little apprehensive about his new environment so was thrilled to discover that I spoke a little Bangla. He felt comfortable telling me that although he was happy with his accommodation, he didn't feel very well since he was not used to the Jordanian diet. He was missing dal bhat, the Bangladeshi staple of rice and beans.

I knew of an Indian restaurant nearby, so we jumped in a car and went to investigate. Not surprisingly, the first item on the menu was dal bhat—he looked so happy I thought he would cry. He immediately sat down to eat and instantly felt at home. His contract was for four weeks, and he went to eat at the Indian restaurant twice a day for the duration of his stay.

Emergency Stash of Treats

•

Bring a survival supply of the treats you crave most. (Resist the temptation to consume them on your flight—which happened more than once in my case.) Hiding a few treats in your luggage is a good idea—out of sight, out of mind. My go-to non-nutritious mood enhancer of choice was M&Ms—with their added bonus of not melting in the heat.

When you are having a tough day or are feeling homesick, such snacks can instantly boost your spirits. In the capital city of whatever country you are volunteering in, you can almost always buy Coke and Mars bars and a few other well-known international brands. If you need a regular fix, find out where you can replenish your stock.

A word of caution, though: cockroaches have the ability to get into any food. While conducting a workshop in rural Bangladesh in March 1995, anticipating that the menu would be limited for my taste buds, I had packed my trusty M&Ms and a package of chocolate-chip cookies, which I was saving for the halfway point in the workshop. On the appointed afternoon, I went to my room to retrieve my prize from a hiding place at the back of the dresser drawer. To my utter dismay, I found that cockroaches had gnawed their way into the pack and eaten some of the cookies. Needless to say, I had to tearfully pitch them all out. Thankfully, I was relieved to see that the tenacious insects were not able to break into the tough plastic bag of the M&Ms. Although I had my heart set on the cookies, the M&Ms provided some consolation.

MANNA FROM HEAVEN!

DATELINE: APRIL 1992 – DHAKA, BANGLADESH. While doing my internship, my flatmates and I had a frugal budget for meals. The spicy meals we had daily were not my cup of tea. I existed by eating a lot of duck eggs on toast and white rice with beans. I didn't complain about it, but I was certainly missing my regular diet.

Four weeks after moving into our apartment, my flatmates and I were having our usual breakfast when one of them announced he had a surprise for us. It was Easter Sunday and like a magician pulling a rabbit out of a hat, he produced a large bag of mini peanut butter cups. He had hidden them in a Tupperware container. Nothing at that moment could have made me happier. When you are far from home, the pleasure of devouring something you love to eat can't be overstated.

DRINKS ANYONE?

By now, the thought may have crossed your mind about where you might have a beer or other alcoholic beverage. When you are immersed in a new culture, having a drink can be a nice way to unwind. Liquor is widely available in most countries, so it shouldn't be hard to locate the local watering hole. Many countries brew beer and locals are always happy when you sample it.

However, in 17 countries around the world with a Muslim majority and in some parts of India, alcohol consumption is strictly controlled and in some cases prohibited, although exceptions are often made for non-Muslims. Unless there is a strict country-wide ban, as in Kuwait or Saudi Arabia, places where Westerners congregate, such as hotels, clubs, and restaurants, often have alcohol available. If local Muslim staff are invited to an event where liquor will be served, it is worth mentioning that in advance; some won't or can't go to an event where alcohol is present, and they would be embarrassed if they had to leave.

Wherever you end up, it is imperative to respect the laws of the country. And to be responsible about your consumption of alcohol. You don't want to embarrass yourself or your hosts in any way. Being a visitor means that you represent your country, whether you want to or not, so consider the consequences of your behaviour. If forgoing a daily visit to the pub isn't conceivable, you will want to consider where your NGO is located.

It is imperative to respect the laws of the country.

INCONVENIENCES IN THE FIELD

To more easily come to terms with your new environment, it's a good idea to anticipate what to expect. If you set expectations low, you won't be disappointed when inconveniences arise, as they are sure to. The following are some circumstances you may find challenging, with suggested solutions:

Heat: High temperatures and humidity can zap your energy and make you feel downright grumpy. Often there isn't the luxury of AC, so adjusting to the heat takes some patience.

Solution: Stay hydrated by drinking a lot! During the day, wear breathable 100%-cotton loose-fitting clothes. At night, moisten a washcloth and place on your forehead or on the back of your neck.

Showers: If a shower is available, there will be limited or no hot water and little pressure.

Solution: Get wet first, use a bar of soap with a washcloth to clean yourself without the water running, then rinse off. When washing your hair, use shampoo sparingly and only once. If there is water in a tank, be economical with its use since it most likely needs to be shared.

Bed: Sleeping on a hard/lumpy/mildewy mattress takes some getting used to, but that is part of the experience.

Solution: Put a sarong or sleep sack over your pillow and sheet to make it feel more comfortable. Use bedbug spray if recommended.

Noise: Without AC, windows need to be open for air to circulate. You will be treated to a variety of night noises that can interfere with getting a good night's sleep.

Solution: Use earplugs.

Mosquitoes et al.: In hot climates, insects are part of the landscape. Cockroaches get into everything, mosquitoes are a constant presence, and lines of small ants seem to appear randomly.

Solution: Pack up any food in a tightly sealed container—leaving food out, even crumbs, is an invitation to a picnic. Use a mosquito net at night. At dusk, wear a long-sleeved shirt and trousers and apply mosquito repellent. At night, if you need to be out, always wear shoes. If your accommodation isn't enclosed, always shake out your shoes before putting them on.

Smoking: In many countries, smoking is still prevalent. If you are accustomed to smoke-free environments, this is an issue that takes getting used to. In many workplaces, smoking is no longer permitted; however, in cafés and restaurants, you can easily find yourself sitting next to a group that lights up just as you begin your meal.

Solution: Check with your host NGO about the smoking policy in the office. When you are eating out, ask if you can sit outside downwind or indoors near good ventilation.

Pollution and sewage: It is easy to take for granted civic garbage collection and underground sewage systems if you are from a wealthy country. Aside from litter, you may find you have to walk over all sorts of waste.

Solution: Be mindful of where your shoes have been—remove them at your accommodation. Practice good hygiene—wash your hands often.

Electricity: You might not have access to power where you sleep, which means you can't charge your devices at night.

Solution: Charge your devices and/or your portable charger in the office during the day and then you can use your charger in the evening. You can also investigate a solar charger.

Lack of privacy: The concept of respecting personal space isn't often adhered to.

Solution: Accept that people will always be looking over your shoulder. Anything you have on display is fair game, so if you don't want people peering at something, put it away.

All of these issues are commonplace. When you first arrive, ask about your bed and bathing facilities. Naturally you will miss some of the creature comforts of home, but it is important to focus on the positive and not complain about the things you find inadequate. Being able to speak to a volunteer who has had experience at your host NGO is your best source of information.

To address all of these challenges, carve out some time to feel grounded. The coping mechanism used by many is listening to favourite playlists, which can immediately take the edge off an unproductive day—you can always rely on music to help get you back on track. Some find meditation helpful. Retreating into a novel is also a wonderful way to leave behind a day's worries. Finally, writing down your impressions and thoughts in a journal is a productive way to process all sorts of new information—with the added benefit of it being a conduit to vent your annoyances.

Carve out some time to feel grounded.

GETTING SETTLED IN THE FIELD
DIARY ENTRY: 17 MARCH 1991 – JONC, HAITI. I woke up at 6:30 a.m. but lounged around under my mosquito net until 7:45 a.m. What a welcome! The bedbugs went to work on my legs last night. I have hundreds of tiny red dots, which I thought were measles at first.

Breakfast was a banana and then I went off to mass with the volunteers who were Catholic. The service at the cathedral in Gonaives in Central Haiti was two hours long, but we missed the first 45 minutes. The pastor of the mission where I'm volunteering didn't pick us up until noon so we had a chance to walk around the market.

Children followed us and were obviously intrigued. The marketplace was bustling with people everywhere. There are no proper stores, just stalls on the sidewalk. There is some hydro eco plumbing (outhouses), and they are all made of bits of tin, mud, and other miscellaneous materials. There are no trees and the heat is unrelenting—stray animals are everywhere. The earth is cracked and rock hard.

I had a rest after a banana lunch, but it was so hot I couldn't sleep, so I just tried not to move. I met with the pastor at 4 p.m. to decide on a plan. The other volunteers are dentists but Roy, another volunteer, and I have to figure out how to be useful.

The meals are already very predictable—either chicken or goat with French fries or rice and beans for dinner. I did find Frosted Flakes in the nearby town, so that will be my breakfast with bananas. I'll be thin in a few weeks—and very hungry! The water seems fine to drink. We have running water for an hour both in the morning and evening. The shower this morning was little more than a trickle, but it is a shower, and the flush toilet not only works, it doesn't smell!

I'm writing by flashlight at 7 p.m.—it is dark by 6:30 p.m. and the sky is spectacular. The mosquitoes are incredibly bad, especially at dusk. I wonder what it'll be like reading with a flashlight—will they swarm around my net or do they go to sleep? I've moved beds so with luck there won't be bedbugs in the other mattress.

❋ ❋ ❋

DIARY ENTRY: 18 MARCH 1991 — JONC, HAITI. It turns out they were small mosquitoes and not bedbugs, so that's a relief. I spent the morning learning about the services at the medical clinic, then went to the house of one of the missionaries to discuss expectations with the pastor and Roy (he's such a know-it-all and already seriously annoying).

Steve, a missionary, took us to the mission store with little inventory, and I wonder who has the money here to buy anything. I tried to rest in the late afternoon but even breathing requires effort in this heat. Before every meal, grace and prayer are part of the program. People are free to make a request to the prayer leader. Tonight, Steve was taking charge so Serena asked if we could all pray for her diarrhea to get better. Steve started the prayer circle and asked us all to pray for Serena to get better so she could do God's work. Words fail me—can't she just take an Imodium?

The beef at dinner was almost tasty. After the meal, I was able to speak to Mum and my boyfriend. It's hard to describe to them what a different world it is here.

HEALTH AND FITNESS

If you like working out on a regular basis, you will have to improvise a fitness routine since going to a gym in rural areas won't be an option. In many cities in developing countries, there are gyms and, in addition, you can investigate clubs that embassy personnel use, which are generally open to citizens of those countries. You can stop by the club with your passport and request an application. Also, many of the larger hotels offer day packages to use their health facilities and pools. Even if you are based in the countryside, it may be possible to plan an excursion on your day off for a swim and exercise. Wearing sports attire—namely workout gear and a bathing suit—are fine within the walls of a club or hotel in the designated areas. Wear appropriate streetwear en route and change into your sportswear upon arrival.

Runners will want to put on their trainers and go for a run. It shouldn't be a problem, but always ask first about a safe route and what clothing is acceptable to wear. For yoga and Pilates enthusiasts, you should usually be able to find a corner on-site to do your stretching and poses.

It can be tempting to throw yourself solely into your work, but overdoing it can lead to burnout. Take time to look after yourself and find a sensible work-life balance.

More than likely your digestive system is going to have some adapting to do. Dealing with diarrhea and constipation is par for the course when you are in a new environment. Just make sure to keep drinking lots of water and eat recommended foods that will help your system adjust.

If and when you do feel ill and your symptoms don't improve in a day or two, your best bet is to stop in at the local pharmacy and ask which medications could cure your ills. Parasites, worms, etc. are annoyingly common in hot climates, but they can be remedied quickly with the correct medicine or antibiotic, often available over the counter. If feeling lousy continues for several days, visit a doctor, who can direct you for tests to determine a diagnosis. In any event, when you first arrive at your host NGO, get the name and contact details of a local doctor who speaks English and add it to your contacts. Ditto for a pharmacy.

> ### *Get the name and contact details of a local doctor who speaks English.*

MAN'S BEST FRIEND—OR FOE?

DATELINE: APRIL 1992 – DHAKA, BANGLADESH. One of my goals during my internship was to make Bangladeshi friends, so I was delighted to be invited to a new friend's home for dinner.

While walking to her front door, her dog came out of nowhere and sunk his teeth into my ankle. I was taken aback and felt tears well up due to the shock of the bite. Her father came rushing out, mortified that a guest had been attacked by the family pet. While a kindly housekeeper tended to my wound, my friend's father assured me that the dog had had its rabies shots and had never bitten anyone in the past.

I composed myself to reassure my hosts even though my ankle was throbbing. I did my best to enjoy dinner with them and then made my way home. When I arrived back at the flat, my flatmates were eating dinner with a friend from the US embassy. When they inquired about my bandaged ankle, they all expressed concern and said I needed to visit a doctor first thing the next day, given that rabies is a serious threat.

The Bangladeshi doctor whom I saw the following morning said the wound didn't require stitches, but I should start the course of rabies shots over ten days right away. When I reported that the dog had been vaccinated, he said I shouldn't take any chances, in case the serum wasn't effective. He gave me my first shot then and there.

In addition, he advised me to inquire about the dog's well-being for the next two weeks. If the dog was still alive two weeks later, it was rabies free—but if it did die, the shots would have been a lifesaver. I secretly went to the doctor's office for my daily rabies shot since I didn't want my friend to take offence. I agreed with the doctor that it wasn't worth taking the risk of getting rabies, but I needed to be diplomatic so as not to hurt my friend's feelings.

WILL MY EARDRUMS EXPLODE?
DIARY ENTRY: 27 MARCH 1996 – SAA FLIGHT FROM JOHANNESBURG TO NEW YORK. Feeling dreadful with a horrendous cold. I am sure my eardrums will erupt. Listening to Handel's *Messiah* in Zulu on the never-ending flight from Joburg in a middle seat trying to get comfortable. A fuel stop at Cape Verde then on to JFK: 17+ hours in total.

I worried about boarding the plane but there were no available flights for another 10 days, so I decided to risk it. I had visions of my head exploding during the long flight over the Atlantic— where could we make an emergency landing?

To my amazement, my seatmate turned out to be a doctor who worked at SC in Westport, CT. That's what I call serendipity! He assured me that my ear infection wasn't life-threatening and my eardrums wouldn't explode. Relieved, I took several painkillers and fell asleep for most of the flight.

IN-COUNTRY TRANSPORTATION

Road accidents are one of the highest causes of death in developing countries, so consider your mode of local transportation wisely. Typically, your host NGO will collect you at the airport, but if not, taxis will be available to take you to your accommodation. Make sure you find out the approximate price of getting from the airport to your hotel in advance and have local currency available to pay.

Uber is unlikely to be available where you are going, or if it is, it likely will only be available in the capital city and not in the countryside. Also, your Wi-Fi might not work, so apps won't be much use, and neither will a credit card.

When travelling by road, avoid getting into rickety vehicles— it isn't worth taking chances. Opt for sturdier transportation and always buckle up. During your stay, taking taxis won't be a feasible or an affordable option if you are travelling with local staff. Your co-workers will inform you about all the various types of minibus taxis, matatus, tap taps, or minivans. When going from a city to smaller towns on public transportation, you will have to be patient since buses don't usually leave until they are completely filled with passengers—and it's incredible how many people they are able to squash in. Smaller vehicles like tuk-tuks (motorized covered scooters) are widely available for short journeys in town. Like taxis, they operate with meters but being open to the elements without much protection, the fare is much lower.

Consider your mode of local transportation wisely.

Traffic can be a nightmare in many big cities, so it may be tempting to hitch a ride on a motorbike or scooter since they can weave in and out of traffic. However, if you do need to use one, be aware of the inherent danger and risk in those manoeuvres, and always wear a helmet. If possible, it is worth paying extra to get from *A* to *B* safely in a bus.

It is easy to get lost in new surroundings, so assume at some point you won't be able to find your way back to your NGO. Don't panic. Upon arrival, get your host NGO's business card and update your contacts list with the name of your host NGO, the address, and a mobile number. Carry the card with you so that if you are lost, you can show it to a taxi driver who can call to get precise directions in the local language.

PERSONAL SAFETY

Take sensible precautions to make sure that you and your possessions are kept safe. Don't take unnecessary risks because anything that happens to you can create a burden to your host NGO. You will get a briefing when you first arrive so heed their advice.

Out on the street, don't flash cash, devices, or jewellery. Drawing attention to yourself by wearing expensive jewellery, showing off your devices, or carrying anything of value out in the open is asking for trouble. Keep a small sum of bills in the local currency in an easily accessible pocket since you don't want to attract notice by flashing money. In the event you are robbed, you can hand over the money in your pocket. Keep the rest of your money safely stored away at your lodgings.

It is always better to go out exploring with a buddy. If you find yourself out and about on your own, try to get a message of your whereabouts to a colleague. When you are on your own in an unfamiliar area, it is preferable to take a registered taxi as opposed to an unregulated private car.

Watch your alcohol intake. Sensible decision-making skills go out the window under the influence of too much liquor. In a bar or pub, never leave your drink unattended. Some drinks could be stronger than you are used to, so go easy when you first arrive. Also, in hot climates, booze can go to your head far more quickly.

And to state the obvious: avoid dark or non-tourist areas at night. Try to stay in a group, but if that's not possible, walk near others so you don't stand out as being alone.

Don't flash cash, devices, or jewellery.

DAILY-LIVING SKILLS

As with other issues in your new environment to which you will have to adapt, ask your host NGO for the best way to handle yourself when you are out in the community.

Negotiating prices: When you are out shopping—not so much for produce in a market but for many non-food items you may want to purchase—negotiating a price is a practiced art. Ideally, ask a local colleague to show you around and advise you about prices. In many cultures, haggling is expected—it is part of the process. Visitors can get obsessed about getting "a good price," but if you have arrived from overseas, paying a higher price than someone local is entirely reasonable.

Responding to beggars: It is heart-wrenching to witness people, especially children, on the street begging. Advocates for poor people advise that you should walk by and not give any money—which is easier said than done. The reason given is that you are encouraging behaviour if you support them, and they will continue to beg. Many beggars are part of an organized network, sometimes part of a mafia operation; the person you intend to help by giving money is often passing it along to a boss behind the scenes. Witnessing some of the conditions people are forced to suffer through is a stark eye-opener.

Tipping: If someone provides you with any type of assistance—carrying bags, serving meals, locating a taxi, etc.—a tip is much appreciated. Likewise, housekeeping staff, bathroom attendants, concierges, hairdressers, tour guides, and drivers will all gratefully receive gratuities.

Providing tips for people who assist you takes on a greater significance in developing countries. Many people are trying to provide for their families on sporadic, low wages. On top of rent and food, there are school fees and health care costs. With little or no safety net, any extra tips can help cover vital expenses. I recommend that you bring a minimum of US$100–$200 for a short stay (and more for a longer stay) for gratuities and to pay local expenses in a market. Saying you don't have money is not how you are viewed, having flown from a faraway country.

PEOPLE WORKING BEHIND THE SCENES

DATELINE: JUNE 1997 – SISOPHON, CAMBODIA. I was on a road trip with my boss, visiting a microfinance program in a rural area in the northern part of the country near the Thai border. On the morning of our departure, I joined him for breakfast and asked him for a few US singles since I only had a $100 bill. He said I didn't need any money since breakfast was included in our rate.

When I explained that I needed the smaller bills to leave a tip in the room for the hotel housekeeping staff, he said that in all the years he had worked for the agency, he had never once left a tip in the room. That he seemed proud of this fact made me very upset. I pointed out that he would tip a waiter who brings a Coke, so it wasn't unreasonable to tip a woman who made his bed and cleaned his bathroom. He defended himself by saying that the hotel pays them.

It infuriated me that someone receiving a generous amount to cover expenses (with incidentals like tipping factored in) wouldn't leave even a small gratuity. It had never occurred to him to leave a tip for a hotel housekeeper. He said I was too generous. I found it ironic that we were in the business of trying to lift women out of poverty with small loans, but he didn't notice poor women doing physically demanding jobs who were not earning even a minimum wage.

Since my experience in Sisophon, whenever travelling, I have made a point of encouraging fellow travellers to leave tips for housekeeping staff.

Something else to consider: at the end of a trip, instead of hanging on to extra notes or coins in local currency, which will only end up at the back of a drawer at home, you can put them to good use. Scout around the airport toilets and locate a bathroom attendant who would be an appreciative recipient of any change or bills. It's a great way to end your trip and such a small gesture can brighten someone's day. Alternatively, you can donate your leftover change on board your flight since many airlines make appeals for spare change, which they contribute to their partner charities.

LEARNING BY EXPERIENCE: TENNIS AT NOON AND CHICKEN FOR DINNER?

DIARY ENTRY: 15 APRIL 1992 – DHAKA, BANGLADESH. Every week, I like going to the American Club where I indulge in a lot of popcorn, pizza, and beer while catching up on ABC news reels read by Peter Jennings. It gives me a feeling of being grounded. The club has a lovely pool and two tennis courts and it's nice to wear a tennis outfit and a bathing suit.

After a swim at midday, I noticed that the courts were empty and so I asked if anyone was up for hitting the ball. A few men who had lived in Dhaka for a while looked amused and said they would be happy to play.

All went well for the first few minutes and then I started feeling peculiar and promptly keeled over. I was carted off to a lounge chair in the shade where I had to spend the afternoon rehydrating, recovering from heatstroke. Needless to say, I was teased for being a rookie and underestimating the heat. I now understood why no one plays tennis at midday—it was a mistake I didn't repeat.

Two of my flatmates are pescatarian so our evening meal consists of "rui mash" (bony river fish that is smothered in curry), dal, and white rice—I stick to white rice and a bit of dal. After getting the OK from my flatmates, I decided it would be a nice idea to have chicken for dinner for a change.

Equipped with basic Bangla, I felt confident enough to go to the local market on my own. When I got to the butcher and asked for chicken, the men nearby gathered round looking puzzled. Unbeknownst to me at the time, chickens are not sold by a butcher, but rather by "a chicken man," who sells his wares from a basket on the top of his head. Someone ran off in search of one, who promptly appeared. He reached up into his basket and handed me a live chicken (with its feet tied together) and told me the price.

How could I explain that I was looking for chicken that was already butchered, plucked, ready to cook, and wrapped in plastic wrap? I paid and thanked him and walked off carrying a live chicken by its feet—trying to look as though this was completely natural. I had no intention of killing it, so when I got close to our apartment, I released it by the slum, where it was caught in a second by an ecstatic resident.

KEY POINTS

1. Brace yourself for squat toilets, adventurous cuisine, and interesting insects.
2. Make yourself aware of inconveniences you might encounter in the field and don't let them get under your skin.
3. Carefully consider your local transportation options.
4. Ask your hosts to recommend a good local doctor, just in case.

Check out the website *amazingvolunteer.com*

1. Jamie provides great tips on how to manage your hygiene while abroad in the video "Travel Hygiene Tips" (SmarterTravel, 2019).

2. Watch Global Citizen's video titled "Access to Clean Water and Sanitation: A Guide to Global Issues" (2016) to familiarize yourself with the realities many people face without clean water.

3. Jess alerts you to travel scams and how to outsmart scammers in the "Most Common Travel Scams" (Mint.com, 2018).

TIME TO GET TO WORK

*The best way to find yourself is to
lose yourself in the service of others.*

– MAHATMA GANDHI

WITH YOUR BASIC living arrangements and meals sorted out, it is time to roll up your sleeves and see what you can learn and how you can be helpful. By way of preparation, before you left home, you should have requested a map, arrival instructions, and any other pertinent details. Being well prepared before you set off saves everyone's time and prevents local staff having to repeat information.

On your first day, you will be given a briefing to help you get oriented to your host NGO and the local environment.

LOOK FOR WAYS TO BE AN ASSET

As a volunteer, the most important asset you bring is a positive approach—and your commitment to maintaining it throughout your stay. Refer back to chapter 4 with regard to how you can be useful now that you are at your host NGO. Work in partnership, define your expectations, and be patient and compassionate. Stick to the fundamental principles of being respectful and open-minded. Gain an understanding of the vision of the NGO, identify responsibilities, and establish lines of communication. Combine that with being a good listener and you will be able to contribute to the work in a meaningful way—your host NGO will be grateful to have you around.

The most important asset you bring is a positive approach.

Taking initiative is typically a welcome trait, but remember that you are new to the country and that your host NGO has been dealing with the issues at hand for decades. Jumping to conclusions or proposing ideas to solve their challenges could be misinterpreted as being arrogant. The NGO has most likely tried every obvious solution, so unless you are asked, it is best not to offer your views. Step back, absorb information, and listen to a variety of people from the area to get a balanced perspective. It takes time but your input can be far more effective if you play the longer game and use a thoughtful approach.

Be a team player. You will have a far greater chance of producing quality results as part of a team than on your own. First impressions are lasting, so park your ego when you arrive. Always be punctual—it is crucial to respect everyone's time. Being a volunteer doesn't give you the right to waltz into the NGO whenever you feel like it.

It is also important to consider making your contribution sustainable in the long term, after you've gone. When you work with a local staff member, pass along any new techniques or skills in a way that enables continuation.

Be a team player. Park your ego.

As a volunteer, *everything* is your job (within reason)! In any assignment, there are aspects that are often mundane but that need to get done. In particular, if you're hoping for an offer of a staff job after your volunteer position, then always be willing to do what you are asked and do it well. Naturally, you shouldn't do anything that is unsafe, so if you ever feel uncomfortable, stand up for yourself and clearly communicate your issue.

GET TO KNOW LOCAL PEOPLE

It isn't enough to sit in the comfort of an office with AC (if you are so lucky!). To get a glimpse of what life is like for the people that your host NGO is serving, you have to get to the field to meet people.

GET OUT THERE!

DATELINE: SEPTEMBER 1993 – SOWETO, RSA. I was conducting a feasibility assessment for CARE to implement microfinance programming in southern Africa and my final stop was Johannesburg. As was customary, a packet of reports was left for me at my hotel so that I could review them in advance of my first meeting.

It was a Sunday, and I had planned to read the contents of the large envelope by the pool. As I started to flip through the documents, it dawned on me that most of them were written by international consultants who likely hadn't even visited Soweto (South Western Townships)—urban settlements created in the 1930s for the black workforce serving Johannesburg. There was some basic information about poor people, their living conditions and economic indicators, but I had no sense of who the people were, what kind of small businesses they ran, or how they lived.

Since I wasn't expected at the office, it was time to go exploring. I asked at reception if I could get a guide to show me around Soweto. It was eight months before Nelson Mandela became president, so the apartheid system had not yet been dismantled, which meant hotels were still segregated. A tour of the neighbouring black township was a novelty, and the staff members looked rather uncomfortable when I made my request.

The concierge did find a leaflet about Jimmy's Bus Tour of Soweto, so Jimmy was contacted and we fixed a time for him to collect me. Jimmy was a tour operator from Soweto and was pleased to have the opportunity to educate people about life in his township.

We started in the marketplace, where a sea of micro-entrepreneurs were selling their wares. Being accompanied by someone local made it easy to speak to market sellers to gain an overview of market conditions, finances available, and obstacles. I enjoyed being in the hive of activity, seeing what people were up to, and getting a feel for the living standards. We walked by the main bus depot with hundreds of matatus (minibuses) destined for rural areas. We visited a couple of houses—people were very welcoming and were keen to tell me their stories and show me their neighbourhood.

After several hours, I returned to the hotel and read over the reports. The next morning, I met with the country office director. When he asked how everything went the day before, I said I had read the information pack he provided and also had taken a tour of Soweto. He was surprised at my impromptu visit to the township since some considered it dangerous. I assured him that I went with a knowledgeable guide and got an excellent field briefing. If we were to establish a program in Soweto, we needed to source reliable first-hand information by speaking to residents in order to identify local partners.

The moral of the story is: for accurate information, always go to the source. Ask people living and working in the community what they think—you don't want to perpetuate incorrect assumptions. However, it is extremely important not to be cavalier. Being accompanied by someone local who is recommended will give you credibility, protection, and help with translation. It is all too easy to wander into a potentially threatening situation to which you may be oblivious.

For accurate information, always go to the source ... people living and working in the community.

Visiting residents in their communities is an enriching experience and one from which you can learn a great deal. Think how you enjoy talking about your life—it is the same for everyone. Many poor people are overlooked, so when an outsider takes an interest, the value of being heard can't be overemphasized. Always make clear that you are a visitor and don't make any promises on the spot. When faced with poverty, it can be tempting to try to fix a situation immediately. Misguided compassion can do damage. Your job is to observe and then take up your questions and concerns with your host NGO. The communities you visit have a long history so it is presumptuous to think you can quickly understand their lives and provide solutions.

Misguided compassion can do damage.

PHOTOS TELL A STORY

DATELINE: JULY 1996 – TBILISI, GEORGIA. I had a contract with United Nations High Commissioner for Refugees (UNHCR) to conduct a study to determine the feasibility of implementing a microfinance program that would meet the needs of refugees. The target group was made up of citizens of Georgia but, within their country, they were referred to as Internally Displaced Persons (IDPs). This came about when conflicts in South Ossetia and Abkhazia (then parts of Georgia) endangered lives causing thousands of families to flee their homes and head to safety in other cities.

I visited market areas in the capital and in other cities and towns around the country, where there was a high concentration of IDPs. I wanted to see what types of businesses they were running and how they were financing them.

Since microfinance was a new idea at the time in the former Soviet Union, I was asked to write a short concept paper to describe people generating income through a variety of activities and explain how small loans could help increase their income. I compiled a series of photographs of microentrepreneurs (always with their permission) selling everything from potatoes out of the trunks of their cars and eggs out of the baskets on their bicycles to household possessions and crafts in market stalls.

The photographs instantly put a face to the intended client group and provided context of how they could be assisted with small unsecured loans. By interacting with the potential clientele of microentrepreneurs, I was able to show who we were trying to target. Walking around the market and talking to prospective borrowers was the only way to obtain this information.

ROLL OUT THE WELCOME MAT

DATELINE: JULY 1996 – TBILISI, GEORGIA. The tough transition from a communist system to a market economy meant that most people now had to eke out a living in jobs they weren't trained for. I had no idea what it was like for someone with an education and a middle-class lifestyle to suddenly become a refugee. I decided it would be useful to have an in-depth conversation over a meal and overnight stay with young people who were forced to flee.

When I proposed the idea to my colleagues, they were dubious. Being a consultant and not a staff member meant I had some flexibility and autonomy. I got the necessary permission and then asked a local colleague to identify IDPs who spoke some English and who would be willing to have me come and stay for a night.

Arrangements were made and I took a taxi—not an agency vehicle, which would attract unnecessary attention—to a rundown hotel where IDPs were being housed. I was advised to bring a "hostess present" of wine and Georgian favourites like meat khinkalis, blinis, and roulettes with walnuts. As a guest, my hosts would have taken offence at being offered money but providing items they would enjoy was a welcome gesture.

Each hotel room housed one family and had to serve as a place to sleep, eat, and bathe. There were no cooking or refrigeration facilities, so the IDPs had to make do with portable cookers and use the windowsill for refrigeration, which was not feasible in the hot summer months. Dishes, clothes, bedding, and bodies had to be washed in one shower stall, almost always without hot water.

My host's room was welcoming and spotless. The three young people who agreed to meet me were all a bit nervous, but sharing a meal and drinks broke down barriers. Finding common ground in enjoying food and wine together led to free-flowing conversation, which isn't possible when you are out in the marketplace conducting a survey to find out about people's financial needs. It was humbling to listen to the stories of my hosts. By and large, they had grown up in comfortable households, gone to school followed by university, and had their lives ahead of them. They took piano lessons, went to plays, attended sporting events—similar to my upbringing in many respects.

As for all too many refugees, returning home wasn't an option for years, which meant they had to take refuge in accommodation provided by the Georgian government. Although they had a roof over their heads, the accommodation was severely deficient and no funds were provided to meet daily expenses for food, transport, education, etc.

With high unemployment in the capital, finding any kind of job was burdensome given that employers favoured hiring locals and not IDPs from another part of the country. Consequently, my hosts started selling cigarettes in kiosks: on a good day, they might earn US$1 or $2. Their parents suffered depression and compensated by drinking heavily to cope with their predicament that had no end in sight.

When describing their lives, they felt ashamed of their current circumstances, hated the stigma attached to being IDPs, and were frustrated at not being able to earn a living using the education they had acquired. None of them wanted to give up, but it was tough dealing with their parents' inability to adapt to the new world of capitalism and the probability that they would not return home. As a community, they needed to support one another and make a plan not only to survive but also to one day thrive in their new surroundings.

Listening to their stories made me grateful for my luck at being born in a safe city in Canada. Having a glimpse of their lives gave me some background and perspective. I tried to imagine what would happen if my family and I had to flee our home, venture to an unfamiliar city where people were hostile, and then try to find a place to stay and some kind of work, all the while watching our savings quickly vanish. Where would we go and how would we survive? Frankly, I couldn't fathom this ever happening. Yet this very same trauma strikes many across the world—who likewise never imagined losing their homes.

Making the effort to connect with people in difficult circumstances certainly left a long-lasting impression on me. Even though I couldn't begin to appreciate their hardships, I was able to have an inkling of the realities they had to deal with on a daily basis. When I wrote the project document to provide financial services to IDPs, my hosts were at the forefront of my mind since I could relate, albeit on a very superficial level, to their needs. But to reiterate, be careful not to make assumptions about a group of people or a country based solely on a couple of conversations with a few people.

YOU HAVE ONE CHANCE AT A FIRST IMPRESSION

DATELINE: 1997 – NEW YORK. At the United Nations Development Programme (UNDP), I managed the MicroStart program. We were hiring a small team of recent MA students from the Columbia University School of International and Public Affairs. For recent graduates, it was a great opportunity to get a taste of being in the UN system with the chance to travel internationally.

One morning, I had scheduled an interview at 8 a.m. but was sidelined with an issue at the office in Uganda. I also had a fax that needed to be sent urgently, so I was trying to figure out how I could deal with the call, the fax, and the interview all at the same time.

When the prospective employee arrived, I hurriedly explained that I was going to have to delay our interview for about 20 minutes—and could I possibly impose upon her to send a fax? She at once agreed, so I gave her a quick set of instructions and positioned her at the fax machine. What a relief! I had the conversation with the director in Kampala and as soon as I was done, the young woman was waiting with a confirmation slip in hand.

We had the interview, but in my mind, she had already proven herself. She was more than willing to do whatever was necessary, demonstrating her ability as a team player from the moment she walked in. She ended up being a superb addition to the team.

I was so pleased with this hiring strategy that I used it for the next candidate. Even though I didn't have an urgent call, I staged the interview exactly as it had gone previously. When I explained my predicament to the candidate and requested that she send a fax for me, she just said, "I don't feel comfortable with that."

Well, I certainly wasn't expecting that response. I pretended to have my call and then went through the motions of interviewing her. I already had a negative impression since she wasn't willing to help out. Not surprisingly, her interview responses amounted to a lot of bragging about how well she had done in her coursework. My recommendation was that we shouldn't hire her, but my boss overruled me because he was impressed with her well-rehearsed sales pitch. True to the first impression she gave, she was not a team player and created tension within our group by letting her personal ambitions get in the way of being collaborative.

LEARN BY DOING

While it is important to read any documentation from your host NGO, the best teacher is first-hand knowledge on the ground.

Adults learn best through experiential learning. Having delivered more than 200 workshops ranging from one day to two weeks, it is interesting to note that the vast majority of learning is done during warm-ups, coffee breaks, and social outings—when people naturally share information. Of all those carefully prepared, perfectly crafted, spell-checked, many-times-revised handouts, only a small fraction of that information is ever looked at again. Reading a handout is simply not how information is most effectively transferred from one person to another. Just think about your shelves and desk drawers. I guarantee that there is a lot of material there that hasn't seen the light of day since the day you collected it—and probably never will. Information is everything, but only when it is shared and applied.

While you are volunteering, if you want to impart any type of skill, demonstrate it. Get the colleague you are training to practice the skill and then encourage them to do it on their own. Just think about learning to drive a car: the only way is to actually drive a car, not talk about driving a car. From my experience working in microfinance, instead of talking about a target clientele, I took colleagues to a marketplace to meet microentrepreneurs. With real life interactions, you can incorporate practical experiences into learning.

ESTABLISH NEW RELATIONSHIPS

Cultivating and nurturing relationships is essential to achieving successful results. In addition, they are the key to having an enjoyable time. The somewhat intimidating reality, though, is that you will be looking to build relationships with people you don't know—yet! You can't force people to engage with you, but more often than not your efforts will result in a meaningful exchange.

The following are some ways and opportunities whereby strangers can become friends.

Name game

First things first: learn the names of your colleagues at your host NGO. We all like to be called by our names, so make it a priority to get to know people's names. In some areas, people might prefer more formality than you are used to. Honorifics are used to convey a level of respect, especially with older people, so check local preferences before jumping in and addressing people by their first names right off the bat. Regardless of what country I'm in or the language spoken, I always ask for the staff list. Seeing the spelling of people's names helps me remember those that are unfamiliar to me. In addition, the list provides an idea of the size of the office and often has the title of each staff member so you know who is responsible for what. If it is a large NGO, learn the names of colleagues in your department. Always introduce yourself to receptionists and drivers—they are at the heart of any NGO and you can bet they have good insider information. I make a game of meeting everyone on the staff list in person. By the end of the first week, I try to tick everyone off the list and often recruit others to help me locate the last few people. Think of the activity as a people treasure hunt.

Learn the names of your colleagues at your host NGO.

Real FaceTime

Bad news for device-dependent people: e-mail and texts are not a way to build relationships! They can be an effective way to confirm plans or meeting times, but using devices is not conducive to working out how to tackle problems or how to deal with any issue at an emotional level. Understanding someone's point of view is best done face to face. This way you can pick up on visual cues and body language to piece together vital information, which is important when dealing with people across cultures. You also have the chance to ask for clarification. "Do you mean to say…" or "I didn't know that you thought…" enables the responder to agree or disagree, which leads to some sort of a resolution in a timely fashion.

In written communication, if a message is composed quickly, the receiver could misinterpret the sender's message, which can lead to a lot of back-and-forth texting. It is easy to correct misinformation in person—often using humour—but typing the wrong thing in a text can lead to incorrect information being transmitted or feelings inadvertently being hurt. Having a conversation can quickly resolve an issue. You might assume that once a text is sent, the receiver has understood it as intended, but all too often, the tone, lack of punctuation, misspelling, or brevity can be misconstrued, leading to further confusion around the intent of the message.

And whether you make a mistake in writing or in person, take responsibility for it and apologize promptly.

Picture perfect
•

Using photos is a great way to make connections with new friends anywhere in the world. Everyone understands familial relationships, so have a photo or two (not 20) easily accessible on your phone to share. Also, people are usually interested in what your city or town looks like. I used to carry a postcard of Toronto's skyline and a Canadian $5 bill with an image of boys playing hockey on it.

Religious inquiry
•

Take time to learn about the main religion(s) that is (are) observed and practiced in your host country. Even if you aren't religious, it is important to always be respectful. People are almost always willing to explain their religion to you, including prayer rituals and moral codes. It can be an enlightening experience to attend a local service as a guest, particularly if it is a holy day or special commemoration.

Holiday happenings
•

When you arrive at your destination, inquire about dates of national holidays and what people do to celebrate or observe them. If you do attend an event, it is always a welcome gesture to bring a cake or treat to participate in a celebration.

It's a home run
•

Sports are a great way of bonding with local people. The importance of sport as a unifying force cannot be overstated. Just as in your country, there will be people who are enthusiastic about supporting a specific team, so ask what sports the local population like to play and watch. Knowing the favourite sports and teams in your host country gives you common ground with new friends. World Cup football is the most popular sport worldwide and even countries that have no team represented have die-hard fans around the world. If you don't already support a team, adopt one and join football mania.

Political savvy
•

Wading into political discourse can cause offence or stir up festering issues. If the topic of politics comes up, it's acceptable to ask questions but avoid making comments about politicians. If things do get heated, change the subject. I always carried sweets with me—"Who would like a mint/chocolate/candy?" is an effective way to cut tension.

Music to my ears

•

Visiting a new country is a wonderful chance to expand your music repertoire. Ask new friends what musicians they like to listen to, and if you can, go and hear local music in a live setting. In my travels, I discovered that the love of popular music sung in English is universal. From ABBA's "Dancing Queen" belted out by a Syrian soldier to Céline Dion's "My Heart Will Go On" played throughout the Caribbean to Tom Jones's "Sexbomb" greeting you in every café, bar, and club in North Macedonia and Bulgaria, you can't avoid whatever English song is top of the charts. Even if the current hit isn't your favourite, it is an easy way to associate with locals. And because it can bring you together, you might find a new appreciation for a song that you had previously dismissed.

BORN IN THE USA

DATELINE: JUNE 1986 – GUILIN, CHINA. During my first trip to China, you were only permitted to travel with a government registered guide. From Hong Kong, I took a tour of Guangzhou and Guilin. My guide spent the majority of his time listening to Madonna's "Like a Virgin" on his Walkman (against the law at the time), which he had received as a present from a previous client. When we got to Guilin, we went to a bar where Chinese music was blaring out of the speakers. The bartender liked having international guests visit his bar, and so when I asked him if he would like to hear the latest in American music, he readily agreed. He replaced his cassette with mine: Bruce Springsteen's "Born in the U.S.A." After the first few chords, everyone went silent, but within minutes we were all singing the refrain "I was born in the U.S.A." It was a wonderful experience to feel a connection with complete strangers. I left the cassette at the bar as a present.

Meal plans

•

Finally, as mentioned in the previous chapter, sharing food is a fantastic way to connect with people from your host country. Enjoying meals with locals and fellow volunteers can often contribute to making new friends.

INTERACT WITH FELLOW VOLUNTEERS

Fostering friendships with like-minded people can be essential for your sanity, especially if you are going through a rough patch. Conversing with empathetic people from a similar culture or from a circle of new local friends can help you get through a low point in the culture shock cycle. Do avoid going down the "everything is better at home" rabbit hole. The grass is always greener when things aren't going your way. Being patient will help you when you are in unfamiliar territory, and having someone hear your concerns can help you find solutions to things that are bothering you.

Romantic Encounters

•

What about romance? Inevitably there are times when people are attracted to one another. Use common sense and be respectful of your local environment and laws. Some conservative cultures are not keen about public displays of affection, so consider what effect your actions may have on the local community. Since you are a visitor, there are always people watching you and making judgments about you. Be wary about your reputation, especially if you are a woman. Also, beware of becoming romantically involved with a local person, which can present a whole range of issues that you might not understand. Flirting and joking might be perceived differently, so use sound judgment. A safe bet is to remain on friendly terms with everyone and avoid romance.

Sadly, for those in the LGBTQ+ community, being gay or trans is still illegal in more than 70 countries, including half of the countries in Africa, 26 Islamic states, 8 Caribbean island states, and 7 in the Pacific, as well as 2 of the former Soviet republics. If you are part of the LGBTQ+ community, you must educate yourself in advance about laws of the country you want to visit so as not to put yourself in any danger or jeopardize the work of your host NGO.

NEUTRALIZE CONFLICT

Don't assume that a shared desire to volunteer overseas will automatically mean you and fellow volunteers are compatible. Working with new colleagues with different motivations and ways of doing things will often create some friction. The reality is, no matter where you go, people can get under your skin, and as anywhere, you have to figure out strategies to work with people who can be incredibly annoying.

Avoiding conflicts that are a regular occurrence in any workplace won't make them go away, so the earlier you address them the better. For some good insights on resolving conflicts, refer to the tips on the following page.

Aim to help create an environment that is open to airing differences in a non-threatening way. Gossiping about people will add fuel to the fire and make any situation worse, so don't fall into the trap.

MY ALTER EGO: THE BHANGTI QUEEN

DIARY ENTRY: MAY 1992 – DHAKA, BANGLADESH. My flatmates and I enrolled in Bangla lessons together for a seven-week course, two and a half hours per day. We would go to our teacher's flat each morning prior to going to our respective internships.

The trip to our teacher's flat was a 20-minute journey by baby taxi (a three-wheeled motorized scooter) from our flat, and the fare was the equivalent of approximately US$1.

Three of us would chip in our 10 taka of the 40-taka fare, but one flatmate never had change, leaving us to pay his way.

The first week, no one minded, but after a while, it was clear he had no intention of paying his share. We were all able to get change during the day, but he simply couldn't be bothered.

Recognizing that his behaviour wasn't going to change unless action was taken, I decided to go to the bank to get change for a few 100-taka notes in 10-taka note denominations. The following morning when he said—on cue—that he didn't have change, I produced 90 taka in small bills and said he would now be able to chip in.

The word for change in Bangla is bhangti—hence my nickname became "the bhangti queen."

....

CONFLICT RESOLUTION TIPS

Clarify what the disagreement is. Control your emotions. Be aware and respect cultural differences. Humour is often a way to point out annoying behaviour.

1. Establish a common goal for both parties.
2. Discuss ways to meet the common goal; agree to talk and establish ground rules. Take turns to talk with no name calling. Listen to the other side. Be quick to forgive.
3. Determine the barriers to the common goal.
4. Agree on the best way to resolve the conflict. Show that you are listening.
5. Acknowledge the agreed-upon solution and determine the responsibilities each party has in the resolution.

....

RESIST BAILING OUT EARLY

At times, there will be difficult moments. Setbacks are to be expected. Remember, you chose to go, so you have to steel yourself and surmount challenges that present themselves. For each problem, power through the obstacles, think rationally, and curb emotions in order to figure a way forward—you will find a solution. Imagine the story you can tell when you have it behind you!

That said, if you find yourself in a situation that is abusive or extremely uncomfortable, by all means you should make a plan to leave. Sometimes situations cannot be resolved. If that is the case, schedule an exit interview. Regardless of how frustrated you may feel, always leave on a good note and don't burn bridges. And you should always provide a sufficient notice period.

KEEP TRACK OF YOUR EXPERIENCES

I highly recommend that you keep a record of your trip in a notebook or at least in your notes section on your phone. You will be visiting lots of new places and meeting many new people. It can be hard to recall names and digest all that you are absorbing and learning every day. Jotting down even basic notes will help you put them into context at a later date. You will discover a lot about yourself; this is a time to think about your own development. Process what you've experienced and apply lessons learned. What do you want to do with your life? What new ideas have you come up with? Without my diaries and faxes to my mother, I wouldn't have written this book!

Process what you've experienced and apply lessons learned.

SEEK ADVICE BEFORE YOU ACT GENEROUSLY

Being a volunteer has built-in responsibilities, including not doing anything that may unintentionally create problems for future volunteers by the examples you set. Without doubt, you will see needs in the communities you travel to, and if you're able, you may want to respond financially. You might think that being generous is helpful, but a simple well-intended action can have far-reaching—and often unplanned, even negative—consequences. Caution is called for.

MAYBE NOT SO HELPFUL AFTER ALL

DATELINE: FEBRUARY 2017 — LAKE TANA, ETHIOPIA. I was travelling with a group of donors to a village to tour a beehive project. Our host NGO had been given a donation in advance of our visit to cover expenses. We got a warm welcome from villagers dressed in their finest, who laid out a feast for us. We sat in a large hut while the bee project was described to us. One donor was suitably impressed, and given that the hives weren't a huge expense, she got up and offered there and then to fund several more beehives. Our village hosts were delighted, everyone clapped, and the donor was thanked profusely. You would think that her action was a positive outcome of our visit.

However, the message received by the villagers was that if they put on their Sunday best, did a dance, and provided hospitality, foreign donors will give money. Our host NGO who introduced us to the villagers was not consulted, so unrealistic expectations were created among the villagers about how the project could develop.

When visiting any kind of project, be an observer, keep your commentary to yourself, and don't make any commitments on the spot. If you want to provide support for a specific need, consult your host NGO before making any promises. That way you'll understand why things are being done the way they are and how your desire to help can best be utilized.

A WELCOME REPLACEMENT

DATELINE: NOVEMBER 2012 – BUJUMBURA, BURUNDI. In a prison that I visited with a donor group, we saw many women and children languishing, waiting for trials. The only source of information and entertainment was a TV, which had broken down. At the end of our visit, I discreetly asked our host NGO if I could pay for a new TV. She spoke to the prison director, who agreed and told me the cost. I had a sufficient amount of dollars, which I gave to our host NGO. I wanted to make a small gesture and was glad to hear from our host that the TV was installed the following day.

Consult your host NGO before making any promises.

SEIZE OPPORTUNITIES

You are in a new country where you are likely to find a plethora of opportunities to learn. Once you are in the field, take the bull by the horns and capitalize on your time in your host country by identifying people you want to meet and programs you want to visit.

Capitalize on your time in your host country.

Given that you made the effort to travel a great distance, you will find that most people are appreciative of your visit and are usually willing to provide you with time and advice. Follow up on all your new leads since you might find inspiration from an unexpected source. It takes energy and initiative to make appointments to see people, but take advantage of the many interesting and inspiring people you wouldn't have had the chance to meet otherwise. Perhaps a person of influence could change your life's direction as Professor Yunus did for mine.

Bear in mind that you may not be back in your host country for a while—so also make the most of exploring as much of it as you can while you are "in the neighbourhood." Muster all the energy you can—you can rest when you go home. Visiting key sights in your host country is also a wonderful way to connect with local residents.

APPRECIATE LOCAL TREASURES

DATELINE: AUGUST 1993 – HARARE, ZIMBABWE. I did a month-long contract for CARE in the southern Africa region. My first stop was Harare, where I was keen to make a good impression. I worked long hours gathering information by visiting market areas, talking to staff members, and reviewing documents in order to come up with suitable recommendations.

On the Friday afternoon of the week I arrived, the friendly receptionist asked what my plans were for the weekend. I earnestly replied that I would work all weekend writing up my report. She said it would be a shame not to visit Victoria Falls, one of the natural wonders of the world: "We have beautiful places to see here, not just slums." She was absolutely right. She said it was easy to arrange a day trip, and within half an hour, my tour for the following day was organized.

On Monday, I was pleased to give her a full report of my visit and how much I loved seeing the spectacular falls, including taking the short "flight of angels" in a small plane. Of course, it was one of the highlights of my trip, but more importantly, it was a good lesson to learn in terms of connecting to local residents and appreciating the places of which they are proud.

PLAN A PROPER FAREWELL

My mother always said, "Leave the party while you are still having a good time." Even if you are more than ready to go home, it is crucially important to leave on good terms. Make time to compose a succinct memo to your host NGO with feedback about your experience. This can be a useful tool in providing direction for the next volunteer who fills your shoes. Ensure that you simply state facts and end with your recommendations. Using diplomacy will leave you in good stead. When asking for a reference, do so several days before departure so your supervisor has sufficient time to fulfil your request on official NGO letterhead.

When travelling, it is fun to meet many new people and visit new places. If you said that you would send a photo, make an introduction, or provide information, make a note on your phone or in your notebook and follow through on those promises. Ideally, do your follow-up daily or weekly, but as much as possible do what you can before you leave the country. The promises you made might not mean much to you, but the people you made them to will be counting on you to keep your word. Leaving a trail of disappointments is not how you want people to remember you.

Say a fitting goodbye to new friends and colleagues. If you can, host a get-together to thank the people who helped you and made you feel welcome. Tie up all loose ends while you are still in the country. When you get home, you will have many demands on your time, so it's important to do all you can before you leave.

*Thank the people who helped you
and made you feel welcome.*

....

A GOOD VOLUNTEER IS...

- Open to learning: Practice keeping your ears open and refrain from dispensing advice.
- Dependable: Commit to being on time and follow through on promises made.
- Humble: Work as a team player and give credit where it is due.
- Empathetic: Be conscious of how your actions could affect others.
- Sensitive to the opinions and experiences of the local people you are there to help.
- Self-reflective: Put learning into action.

....

THAT'S A WRAP

FAX TO: Elizabeth Gibson, Toronto, Canada
FROM: Susan Gibson, Dhaka, Bangladesh
DATE: 4 July 1992

Dear Mum,

On 19 June, I returned from a splendid eight-day trip to Nepal. In order to renew my visa, I needed to leave Bangladesh, so it was the perfect excuse to make a side trip to Nepal for the first time. The Himalayas were breathtaking—I even was able to take a flight around Everest! I loved white-water rafting and riding on an elephant where I had a bird's-eye view of eight rhinos. Kathmandu was a backpacker's paradise with lots of great scenery, inexpensive restaurants, excellent shopping, and a fun atmosphere.

This is my last dispatch from Bangladesh since I'm set to leave Dhaka on 16 July. I like it here very much; however, my enthusiasm for the new and different has waned. The appealing aspects of the new culture became overshadowed by some frustrations. Here are my top six challenges:

1. Health: My system has not adapted as well as I had hoped. I had a recurring parasite, which is now under control. Aside from other various and interesting ailments, I was bitten by a dog and had to have a series of post-exposure rabies shots.

2. Bangladeshi food: This is not the place to be a fussy eater. Food affects my mood more than I care to admit. During the week, the woman who cooks for us made us the same fish and spicy vegetable dish every night, so I opted for plain rice and dal.

3. Being cut off from home: I didn't receive any mail for two months. I think someone found a single North American woman's mail interesting, but I wasn't able to find where it disappeared to.

4. Living situation: The bugs, mildewy mattress, and lack of furniture does not endear me to my new domicile. Even with ceiling fans, the heat makes it hard to sleep so I often feel crabby.

5. Lack of privacy: As a foreign woman, I'm stared at constantly, and there is no privacy in anything you do.
6. Male attitudes: I'm fed up with inappropriate comments from Western men I've met here. Most are married whose wives aren't here.

I have learned that it is more difficult than it appears to adapt to a new culture and living situation. Having said all of this, I have learned so much at Grameen Bank and feel fortunate that I had this opportunity. I've been exposed to countless new experiences—many that I could never have imagined—and met many fascinating individuals who are making valuable contributions to try and tackle poverty-related issues. I hope that I can take what I've absorbed and find a niche at home where I can do something worthwhile. Overall, it has been the experience of a lifetime.

I've thoroughly enjoyed making new Bangladeshi friends through Grameen Bank and my English classes. We discussed many different topics that gave me an insight into their culture as well as my own. Subjects we covered included: foreign aid, marriage, dating, divorce, MTV, baseball, dieting, alcoholism, and malpractice insurance. At times it was challenging to explain certain aspects of my culture. For example, they thought it incomprehensible that people would want to sit in the sun to make their skin look darker.

The things I'll remember most about Bangladesh are the hospitality; the importance of family; the friendly, kind people; the lushness of the land; palm trees; exquisite flowers; rickshaws; colourful saris; sensational night skies; monsoons; and the will of the people to never give up.

I'm glad I will be staying with you until I figure out what happens next. I do have to start my thesis as soon as I get back. I can hardly wait to see you! Love, Susie

HOMEWARD BOUND

DIARY ENTRY: 20 JULY 1992 – BANGKOK, THAILAND. I'm all set to fly halfway around the world. The check-in attendants were very helpful. It was a good thing that I'd bought an extra-large storage bag because it could hold both my backpack and my new jute carpet. It's amazing to think that in the next 24 hours I'll be in Taipei, Seoul, Vancouver, and Toronto.

It'll be a strange feeling to be home again. I don't know what the future holds, but I'm eager to take on whatever new challenges come my way. I don't know whether I'll end up getting married, working in Toronto, or what will happen. I am feeling optimistic about the future.

What an experience I've had in Bangladesh and how much I've learned. I wouldn't say that I've changed, but my horizons have definitely been broadened. What I'm wearing now—a new T-shirt and 10-year-old trousers—seems to sum up the way I feel. I'm still the same but have a fresh perspective on top of my fundamental outlook.

KEY POINTS

1. Be on time, be flexible, and offer to help.
2. Get out and meet people; communicate with local residents and learn from their experiences.
3. Invest time in getting to know new colleagues and fellow volunteers.
4. Keep a journal where you can document your experiences, vent your frustrations, and note new ideas.

Check out the website *amazingvolunteer.com*

1. Adam provides tips on making a positive, lasting impression in the video "Why First Impressions Last a Lifetime" (The Lavin Agency of Speakers Bureau, 2016).
2. Watch the TEDx Talk where Jonathan emphasizes the importance of listening leading to impactful change: "Shut Up & Listen—Locally Focused Community Driven Solution— Jonathan Kline—TEDxKalamazoo" (2019).
3. Watch "Nelson Mandela's Iconic Speech: Sport Has the Power to Change the World" (Laureus, 2020).

Part 4

....

REAJUSTING TO LIFE BACK HOME

RETURNING HOME AND NEXT STEPS

There is nothing like returning to a place that remains unchanged to find the ways in which you yourself have altered.

– NELSON MANDELA

RETURNING FROM OVERSEAS can be a much-anticipated, albeit somewhat uncertain, phase. You will be happy to return to familiar surroundings and the creature comforts of home, and you will be keen to see family members and friends to relay tales from the country and environment you have visited. Experiencing mixed emotions while you adjust back on your home turf is completely normal so give yourself time and space for the re-entry period.

SEEING A WHOLE NEW WORLD

When I returned home after my trip to Haiti in 1991, I found it remarkable to flip a switch and have light and to turn on a tap and get clean, safe water. Before my trip, I had taken for granted that there was a reliable source of electricity and clean water. Even though I had been away for only a couple of months, a short period of time in a developing country teaches you that for many people, that is not the case. Going to a grocery store on my return also had an impact on me. The sheer volume and selection of *stuff* available (85 varieties of cereal!) was a bit overwhelming, and it made me feel guilty.

Being back in a country with such obvious excesses can take a little getting used to. Surprisingly, although you may have found some things irritating about where you were staying, you may well come to appreciate the virtues of a less materialistic and uncluttered way of life. Practicing gratitude for the things you have and considering the inequality in your home country is a healthy result of being away.

RECONNECTING AND SHARING

For most of us, reuniting with our family and friends will be a happy occasion. But be sensitive to the fact that most people will grasp only a fraction of what you have experienced; don't be disappointed when they fail to share your enthusiasm or dwell on less relevant aspects of your journey. You will have had a unique opportunity and gained a new perspective about a different way of life in a new culture. More importantly, you will have expanded your worldview. Dealing with the attitudes of some people who have not had your experience or who have a narrow view of the world can be frustrating. Have patience. You can't change their views—you can only hope to enlighten them.

When sharing highlights of your journey, I recommend taking the time to distill your volunteer stories into an elevator pitch. You are now an unofficial ambassador for the NGO and country you visited and a conduit of information to people who otherwise might not know anything about it. Family and friends who are genuinely interested will ask you further questions. You will likely be attracted to others who have also taken the plunge into the volunteer world. Investigate social media groups that you can join to continue discussing your interests.

Distill your volunteer stories into an elevator pitch.

APPLYING WHAT YOU'VE LEARNED

Volunteering overseas can set you apart from those who haven't been in the field. With your trip fresh on your mind, this is the moment to process your time away and start to figure out what comes next. Think about how you could further your learning and fill in gaps in knowledge. Sharing information is key to working in partnership and to potentially getting a job. Make a list of people you know who might be interested in hearing about your experience and then offer to give a briefing at a book club, a community centre, or a university class. You never know where taking initiative will lead.

In my case, I followed up on a contact at Scotiabank that I heard about while at Grameen Bank. My connection to the bank was an asset, but it was my field experience and follow-up that secured a short-term job. Knowing there was interest on the bank's part, I made an appointment and prepared a brief presentation about my internship. To my delight, I was offered a job to conduct a study to gauge the feasibility of a microfinance program at the bank. The success of the research and proposal led to a renewal of my contract to implement a microfinance program called Scotia Enterprise, a full-fledged product of Scotiabank, located in Georgetown, Guyana. Ten months after I started my contract, I received a letter from the Government of Canada acknowledging our work with an award. It was a team effort, so we all celebrated. Many employers value employees who propose initiatives and offer solutions. Even if they aren't exactly the right solution, it demonstrates you are a risk taker and not afraid to fail by coming up with new ideas.

THAT WORKED OUT RATHER NICELY...

FAX TO: Susan Gibson
FROM: André Ouellet, Minister of Foreign Affairs, Ottawa, Canada
DATE: 8 June 1994

As the Minister responsible for the Canadian International Development Agency, I am pleased to extend my congratulations to you for your outstanding contribution to Scotiabank's Scotia Enterprise in Guyana, an endeavour that earned your company the 1994 Canadian Award for Private Sector Contribution to International Development in the industrial co-operation category. It is the expertise, enthusiasm, and dedication of employees that make a company a success. You must feel a great personal sense of satisfaction knowing that your work has brought benefits to the people of Guyana and of Canada.

Canadian Awards for International Development 1994. The inscription on the award reads: For a project that has contributed to the creation of long-term business links and in recognition of its outstanding commitment in the creation of a credit facility for microentrepreneurs in Guyana, SCOTIABANK is awarded a Canadian Award in International Development, sponsored by Northern Telecom, presented during the 11th Annual CEA/CIDA Consultations in Hull, Canada, on 8 June 1994.

Congratulations for your good work and best wishes for the future.

Sincerely, André Ouellet

FOLLOWING UP AND STAYING IN TOUCH

Once you've unpacked, it's time to get in touch with all the new contacts you made along the way. From my experience, some of those contacts can become long-term friends, but you have to invest time and effort in cultivating them. You are only as good as your follow-up—if you've made promises to keep in touch with anyone, make sure you honour any commitments made. When someone is kind enough to make time for you, it is important to send a note of thanks the same day or the following day—not in a week or two. And if one of their suggestions helps you in some way, send them a quick update. It is always heartening to receive good news from people to whom you have given advice. Very few people keep in contact with interesting developments—an e-mail providing a positive update with no request for anything in return is a novelty. Being proactive takes time, but it distinguishes you from the multitude of jobseekers.

You are only as good as your follow-up.

Sometimes you will be asked to give guidance or advice. When you meet with a new contact and go on to provide information, make an introduction, or even buy a drink or meal—do it without the expectation of anything in return. Thinking that someone should repay you in some way is transactional and can lead to disappointments.

WHAT'S NEXT?

Once you get re-rooted back home, you may feel somewhat anxious about not having an idea where the road will lead and what decisions lie ahead. Allow yourself the mental space to let your overseas visit settle and then see how you feel.

For many people, volunteering overseas will be a one-off enriching experience. However, if you yearn for more, be advised that it may take time for your aspirations to become clear and focused, and for your plans to coalesce. Keep an open mind about your future and don't worry about what critics say about not following a conventional path.

When following your passion, you open yourself up to criticism, notably from people who avoid risk taking. Find a like-minded group of friends who will provide you with encouragement. Invest your time in further research and follow up on leads—and you might find that new opportunities present themselves in unlikely places.

GIVING CREDIT WHERE IT'S DUE

FAX TO: Elizabeth Gibson, Toronto, Canada
FROM: Susan Gibson, Save the Children, Tete, Mozambique
DATE: 17 March 1996

Dear Mum,

I am in Tete, the northern part of Mozambique, near the borders of Malawi, Zimbabwe, and Zambia—this was a centre for repatriating refugees after the war ended. I'm staying in a guesthouse with AC, which is comfortable. Tete is synonymous with heat, and there are quite a few creepy crawlies around so I'm glad to have a mosquito net. I went to the field today to look at the possibility of implementing a lending program for young carpenters who have been trained at a workshop funded by SC.

I've been thinking about the last five years. I left the United Way in March 1991 to go to Haiti. I don't remember the exact order of events that prompted my departure from Toronto, but I do know that when I proposed the idea of going away for a while, you recognized my restlessness and encouraged me to go.

You've been supportive of all my endeavours since then, even when it meant my travelling to some remote places around the globe and when it was not entirely clear what my next step would be. I feel lucky to have found a profession for which I have a passion and one that takes advantage of my interests in travelling, banking, training, and people. Your keen interest in microfinance combined with your economic background have been invaluable in helping me produce practical documents that have been useful, most of all to field staff.

I've had the chance to visit many different countries (50!) and have gained a perspective that I never would have dreamed of. I hope that I can continue to use these experiences to convince banks and donors that investment in the microenterprise sector is worthy of their attention.

I am grateful for your support in pursuing a career off the beaten track, and I am glad I didn't settle for less. I just wanted you to know that I always tell people what a great mother I have and thought perhaps I should tell you too!

It would be lovely if you came to New York for several days before I disappear again. I might go to Jamaica for three weeks in mid-April to train the new staff of a microfinance program financed by the Dutch and Jamaicans. What about coming in early April? I have some free time, and although I have to write a report for the State Department, it's not due for a couple of weeks. The weather will be nice by then, and we could see the Maria Callas play, visit the Brooklyn Museum, look at Fabergé eggs at the Met—whatever you like. Love, Susie xo

ARE YOU ON BOARD?

It takes a lot of effort and initiative to make a good plan to go overseas to volunteer. You want to aim for an end result that has both you and your host NGO agree: "That was really worthwhile!"

You will make mistakes along the way—that is experiential learning at its best. However, if you are well prepared, you can avoid making some amateur errors and be an asset to a local NGO. Researching and preparing in advance can drastically alter the purpose and outcome of your visit and will increase your chance of having a successful trip. You will have an idea of what to expect, be positioned to learn, and ultimately be useful. If all goes well, both you and the NGO will have a mutually beneficial and rewarding experience, and you will make new lifelong friends.

CONCLUDING LESSONS

I am no longer a consultant and my visits to the field are less frequent. However, the memories and experiences have left indelible impressions and inform how I continue to interact with NGOs. Being involved in international development is a never-ending work-in-progress. Each visit enhances your perspective, but learning is ongoing.

The main lessons I learned from the field are:

1. **Be prepared:** Do your research. Being informed positions you to have a worthwhile experience.
2. **Spend time in the field:** Don't just talk about it—do it. You've gone to all that trouble to get on a plane and put yourself out there, so now make the most of it. Interacting with local people will help clarify what their needs are.

3. **Respect people:** Poor people are survivors—don't patronize them. You are a guest in a country, so behave with grace and modesty. Be on time.

4. **Listen:** Work on really listening to what people are communicating to you, not what you assume they will say.

5. **Learn by doing:** You don't know all the answers, especially if it's a first visit for you. Test and reconsider your assumptions and don't jump to conclusions.

6. **Work in partnership:** Collaboration is the most effective way to achieve lasting results. Invest time in establishing relationships with local residents. Be a catalyst, a cheerleader, a facilitator, and a connector.

7. **Connect with the local NGO staff:** Make an effort to interact with everyone at your host NGO—find out about your colleagues' lives.

8. **Park your ego:** Do the most good and be the most useful you can. Don't set out to take credit for the things you accomplish. Leave the back-patting to family and friends. It's not all about you!

9. **Be adaptable:** Put yourself in other people's shoes and be empathetic.

10. **Follow up:** Promptly thank anyone who has helped you. When you make promises and commitments, keep them.

To be really useful as a partner in development takes humility, effort, and compassion. Ultimately, it is a privilege to play a supportive role to local leaders and NGOs in the field to effect change from the grassroots up. Applying these principles will lead to a truly rewarding experience where you can both learn and be helpful.

EPILOGUE

The most difficult thing in the decision is to act.
The rest is merely tenacity.

— AMELIA EARHART

SOMETIMES, THERE IS a convergence of good luck and being at the right place at the right time that culminates in a positive outcome. A series of events took place in March 2014 that led to a fruitful outcome that I wouldn't have thought possible.

MARCH 2014: KURDISTAN

In 2001, having been based in New York for seven years, I got married and moved to London with my husband. After ten years of working overseas, I wanted to spend more time at home with my husband and our son in our new city. I chose a new path, using my field experience to volunteer on a few NGO committees and boards in the human rights, girls' education, and refugee sectors.

As a board member of the International Rescue Committee (IRC) UK, a small group of us visited Jordan and Iraq in March 2014. The war in Syria had started three years earlier, and the refugee situation had reached devastating proportions, with

more than four million refugees crossing borders into neighbouring countries.

We visited the Zaatari refugee camp, north of Amman, Jordan,
where 60,000 refugees were living in bleak conditions. We then
flew to Northern Iraq, landing in Erbil, the unofficial capital of
Kurdistan, and drove northwest to Dohuk, where many Syr-
ians had taken refuge. We visited programs in urban areas as
well as in the nearby Domiz and Gawilan camps. The quality of the programs in health, education, women's protection,
water, and sanitation was impressive. In addition, the IRC staff
used a participatory approach that involved refugees in decisions
about how programs could best be implemented to adapt to their
needs.

On the night prior to our departure from Kurdistan, we
were treated to a BBQ in Dohuk with IRC colleagues and
staff from partner NGOs. After a few drinks, the country rep
dropped the bombshell that a decision from UNHCR had been
reversed. She had put on a brave face while showing us around,
but in reality, she was filled with apprehension, unsure how
she would meet the payroll the following week. She went on
to explain that, although she had a signed agreement with
UNHCR, a change in local personnel meant priorities had been
restated.

I said I knew only one person at UNHCR, Emmanuel Gignac,
with whom I had worked in Georgia almost two decades earlier.
I hadn't been in touch with him since, but as luck would have
it, he had just moved to Erbil and was now heading up UNHCR
in Northern Iraq.

18 YEARS EARLIER: TBILISI, GEORGIA

Flashback to January 1996, when I was hired by the Bureau of Population, Refugees, and Migration (PRM) at the US Department of State. I travelled to Armenia, Azerbaijan, and Georgia to assess the feasibility of microfinance programming. After the breakup of the Soviet Union in 1989, the Caucasus region was in turmoil due to localized conflicts, resulting in large displacements of people in all three countries. Emergency funding had been in place for several years, but donors were now looking for alternatives that would enable people to rebuild their lives.

Although it was my first visit to the region, I did have exprience in microfinance, which could be an attractive option for NGOs to consider. When I arrived, I met many NGO representatives who were worried about diminishing grant sources—they were looking for alternative programming that could attract new funding. I visited income-generating programs in all three countries and compiled findings, with suggestions about how microfinance could be a way of supporting IDPs who were forced to flee their homes.

In Georgia, I met Emmanuel, who was then a program officer for UNHCR. He liked the idea of shifting the focus from a handout mentality to providing small loans so that people could earn income. Several months later, he offered me a five-week contract in Georgia to conduct an assessment and design a microfinance program that UNHCR could support. I returned a month after I submitted my report to lead a kick-off workshop. My job came to a natural conclusion and I moved on to the next assignment, never knowing how things turned out since e-mail was not widely used at that time.

BACK TO MARCH 2014: KURDISTAN

The IRC country rep couldn't believe that I knew the person who was now the decision-maker at UNHCR in the regional head-quarters in Erbil. What were the chances?!? I had lost touch with Emmanuel, so she gave me his e-mail address and I sent him a message. Within the hour, I had an enthusiastic response from him, and we agreed to meet the following day in Erbil. Although my IRC colleagues were keen to accompany me, I wanted to reconnect with Emmanuel before discussing the funding situation.

It was as though I had seen Emmanuel yesterday. We had a happy reunion over what turned out to be a three-hour coffee. We enjoyed reminiscing at length about the "good old days" in Georgia. It turned out that the microfinance program that I had designed was still going strong.

After bringing each other up to date about spouses, kids, and travels, I told him about the IRC board trip. Since he had just taken on his new post, I didn't expect that he knew the details of funding contracts in the region. I requested that he take a look at the agreement with IRC, to see if the funding priorities had in fact changed and if so, could he consider a transitional funding period of three to six months so that IRC could secure other means to cover expenses. I emphasized that time was of the essence, so he said he would meet with the country rep the following week.

DAYS LATER: LONDON

Once back home, I stayed in touch with both the country rep and Emmanuel to make sure nothing fell through the cracks. Five days after returning from Kurdistan, an IRC (UK) board meeting was held. One of the agenda items was the US$2-million funding issue in Kurdistan. Over the phone, the regional director reported that as a result of the board's trip to the region, there might be some room to revisit UNHCR's position because there was a new head in place. I was duly recognized for my involvement. Within ten days, the funding IRC needed to continue its program in Kurdistan had been reinstated.

What an unexpected, well-timed coincidence. It is hard to fathom that being a consultant in Georgia in August 1996 and subsequently participating in a trip to Jordan and Iraq in March 2014 could have such a positive conclusion.

🍁 🍁 🍁

My desire to volunteer overseas evolved into a career of learning, sharing information, and being a conduit of resources. Working with many dedicated people around the world has given me much joy in my life. I hope you too might choose a path that finds you embarking on a worthwhile adventure to be of service.

RESPONSIBLE VOLUNTEERING

THE FOLLOWING COMES from the International Citizen Service (ICS) and is reprinted with their permission.

WHAT IS RESPONSIBLE VOLUNTEERING?

Responsible volunteering projects are based on the needs, priorities, and aspirations of communities where they take place, and delivered in collaboration with the community, with sustainability in mind. They are responsibly managed to ensure the safety and well-being of the community as well as of volunteers.

The most impactful volunteering projects work because they've been designed in such a way that volunteers add real value, rather than engaging in superficial or dangerous work. Otherwise, volunteers may find themselves doing work they are unqualified and unprepared for—or inadvertently taking away a job a local person could do.

VOLUNTEERING OVERSEAS: THE CHECKLIST

At ICS, we want you to make an informed choice about the type of work you choose to undertake as a volunteer overseas. Here are some key questions to keep in mind before choosing an organization to volunteer with.

Does the organization …
- work with local partners?
- provide training before you go?
- provide support through experienced local staff?
- provide medical insurance?
- ask you to fundraise? If so—where does the money go?
- explain the value of using international volunteers?
- have a long-term plan for the communities they support?
- conduct safeguarding checks for volunteers who work with children?
- offer you the opportunity to talk to volunteers who have been on placement?

PACKING LIST FOR A HOT COUNTRY

Clothing

Underwear (cotton)

Sleepwear

Socks

T-shirts (avoid plunging necklines and sleeveless shirts—seeing underarms is too much info)

Long-sleeved shirt (wear in evenings to protect arms from mosquitoes)

Lightweight trousers ("pants" in many countries means underwear), such as cargo trousers with zipped pockets

Jeans (only one smart pair—ones with holes are not appreciated in many countries; jeans are often too hot to wear on a regular basis)

Sweater/fleece (planes or air-conditioned offices are often chilly)

Sports gear (shorts, yoga pants, and tops—but only wear where appropriate)

Sandals

Running shoes (with good tread to avoid slipping on muddy
   surfaces)

Flip-flops (for shower areas)

Bathing suit with cover-up

Rain jacket

Sun hat/baseball cap

Sarong—large pieces of cotton fabric (an impromptu skirt, a
   top layer sheet if you are unsure about the bedding, or a
   picnic sheet)

Lightweight jacket with inside pockets to carry valuables

Women:

Bras

Loose-fitting dress and skirt

Long scarf or sarong (to cover your head in a place of worship,
   protect your arms from the sun, wipe away sweat, and use
   as a dust cover for your laptop)

One smart outfit: longish cotton dress or skirt and top with
   jacket

Men:

Undershirts

Long shorts (many countries frown upon men wearing shorts)

One smart outfit: Polo T-shirt (with a collar) and khaki
   trousers, belt, and tie

Toiletries (travel sizes if your trip is two weeks or less)

Toothbrush/toothpaste/dental floss

Soap

Shampoo/conditioner

Deodorant

Face cleanser/moisturizer

Shaving cream/razor

Sunscreen

Insect repellent

Brush/comb

Contact lenses/solution

Feminine hygiene products (hard to get tampons in rural
areas)

Nail file/clippers/tweezers

Hair ties

Makeup (minimal!)

Birth control/condoms

Vitamins

Prescriptions—get any meds you need for the duration of the
trip (keep a doctor's note for any prescription drugs)

First-Aid Kit

Ibuprofen (Advil) and paracetamol (Tylenol)

Waterproof bandages/blister plasters

First-aid ointment

Rehydration salts

Diarrhea tablets

Iodine or a SteriPen (to purify water)

Miscellaneous

Extra face mask(s)

Hand sanitizer

Toilet paper

Travel tissue packs (can also be used as toilet paper)

Travel umbrella

Fold-up tote bag

Mosquito net

Small flashlight and/or headlamp (using a flashlight saves the battery on your phone)

Ear plugs

Extra batteries

Collapsible cup and spoon

Laundry soap/laundry bag

Microfibre towel and washcloth

Sleep sheet (a sarong will also serve this purpose)

Tupperware container (protects anything tasty from ants, etc.)

Several sturdy plastic bags or pouches (for wet clothes, shoes)

Several zip-lock baggies

Useful extras: Scotch tape, duct tape, bag clips, clothes pegs, rubber bands

Snacks: muesli or energy bars

Small presents for hosts/kind people who help you. Suggestions include small photo calendars, pens, hard candies (avoid chocolate since it easily melts), Body Shop soaps (colourful and practical), and books (which you can read then leave behind)

Carry-On: Valuables

In a crossbody bag:

Passport (with visas and introductory letter if needed)

Smart phone

Washable face mask

Travel wallet with only (take out all loyalty cards/membership cards, etc.):

Cash

Driver's licence (plus an international one)

Credit cards (ideally Visa and Amex)

ATM card

Travel insurance card

In Case of Emergency (ICE) card (that includes emergency
contact number, next of kin, blood type, allergies, etc.)

In your backpack:

Notebook (to jot down notes, as well as a backup for important
information on your phone, like key phone numbers and
itinerary)

Laptop or tablet

Charger and adapter

External battery charger—ideally with a solar feature

Headphones (plug-in ones don't require charging)

Camera with memory card

Eye wear (spare pair if you can't see without glasses)

Sunglasses

Printed copies (stored in a plastic letter-size folder):

*Note: Save all of these documents on a USB memory stick to
bring for additional backup.*

Itinerary

List of emergency contacts and in-country contact list

Copy of main passport page (in the event of loss—call
immediately!)

Credit-card/bank contacts (in the event of loss or theft—call
immediately!)

Copy of travel insurance policy

Resumé (C.V.)

International Certificate of Vaccination booklet (WHO format)

Birth certificate (copy only—useful to apply for additional visas)

Passport photos (for additional visas or identity card)

Maps/directions

Criminal record clearance (often needed when working with vulnerable groups)

Other items:

Book (trade it after reading) or e-book

Guidebook

Shawl (use as a wrap or blanket)

Empty water bottle (fill post-security) ·

Notebook/pen

Note: While the following items are already packed in your checked bag, it's handy to include small portions in your carry-on.

Change of clothes (in case your luggage goes missing)

Tissues

Lip balm

Travel-size hand sanitizer

Snacks

Small supplemental toiletry kit containing prescription drugs needed for a couple of days, ibuprofen (Advil) and paracetamol (Tylenol) (in case of headache, muscle pain, cold symptoms while travelling), toothbrush, toothpaste, deodorant, and moisturizer

GLOSSARY

AUB American University of Beirut

BVES Bureau pour le Volontariat au service de l'Enfance et de la Santé

CRS Catholic Relief Services

developing country A country with a gross national income (GNI) of less than US$12,000—there are 133 countries in this category. Another term used is less developed country (LDC). The term "LDC" can naturally seem hierarchical and/or patronizing as was the term "Third World," which is no longer used. The term "Global South" has been adopted by the World Bank but is inaccurate given that Australia and New Zealand are geographically in this group and have much higher GNIs. Haiti has a low GNI and is in the Global North.

FGHR Fund for Global Human Rights

grassroots The most basic, fundamental level of an organization, providing solutions to local problems

ICS International Citizen Service

IDP Internally Displaced Person

in the field Literal meaning: away from the office. In development or humanitarian terms, it means to be engaged in practical work in a country emerging from a conflict or emergency situation.

IRC International Rescue Committee

ISO International Organization for Standardization

MDG Millennium Development Goals

microcredit Loans, typically ranging from US$20 to US$1,000, made available to low-income people who aren't able to access loans from a bank

microfinance Financial services, including loans, savings, and insurances, made available to low-income people who otherwise don't qualify in the formal banking sector

microentrepreneur An owner and operator of a very small business

microenterprise A small business employing nine or fewer people

MSF Médecins sans Frontières (Doctors Without Borders)

NATO North Atlantic Treaty Organization

NGO Non-governmental organization; voluntary sector, not-for-profit sector and non-profit sector, or charity also used in the same context

SC Save the Children

SDG Sustainable Development Goals

SHOFCO Shining Hope for Communities

TOEFL Test of English as a Foreign Language

UN United Nations

UNDHA United Nations Department of Humanitarian Affairs

UNDP United Nations Development Programme

UNHCR United Nations High Commissioner for Refugees

VPN Virtual private network

WWB Women's World Banking

BIBLIOGRAPHY

Bennett, Claire, Joseph Collins, Zahara Heckscher, and Daniela Papi-Thornton. *Learning Service: The Essential Guide to Volunteering Abroad*. Dorset, England: Red Press Ltd., 2018.

Bornstein, David. *How to Change the World: Social Entrepreneurs and the Power of New Ideas*. New York, NY: Oxford University Press, 2007.

Covey, Stephen R. *The 7 Habits of Highly Effective People: Powerful Lessons in Personal Change*. New York, NY: Simon & Schuster, 2020.

Lonely Planet. *Volunteer: A Traveller's Guide to Making a Difference around the World (Lonely Planet Travel Reference)*. Footscray, VI: Lonely Planet, 2013.

Lough, Benjamin J. "A Decade of International Volunteering from the United States, 2004 to 2014." Washington University in Saint Louis. Center for Social Development, George Warren Brown School of Social Work, March 2015. https://openscholarship. wustl.edu/cgi/viewcontent.cgi?article=1014&context=csd_ research.

Papi, Daniela. "Viewpoint: Is Gap Year Volunteering a Bad Thing?" BBC News. BBC, 1 May 2013. www.bbc.com/news/magazine-22294205.

Participate Learning. "The 4 Stages of Culture Shock." Medium. Global Perspectives, 11 March 2019. https://medium.com/global-perspectives/the-4-stages-of-culture-shock-a79957726164.

Roosevelt, Eleanor. "Statement to the United Nations' General Assembly on the Universal Declaration of Human Rights

(1948)." Statement to the United Nations' General Assembly on the Universal Declaration of Human Rights (1948) | Eleanor Roosevelt Papers Project | The George Washington University. Accessed 4 September 2020. https://erpapers.columbian.gwu. edu/statement-united-nations-general-assembly-universal-declaration-human-rights-1948.

United Nations. "Sustainable Development Goals." UNDP. Accessed 4 September 2020. www.undp.org/content/undp/ en/home/sustainable-development-goals.html.

United Nations. "United Nations Millennium Development Goals." United Nations. United Nations. Accessed 4 September 2020. www.un.org/millenniumgoals/.

Yunus, Muhammad, and Karl Weber. *Creating a World without Poverty: Social Business and the Future of Capitalism*. New York, NY: PublicAffairs, 2011.

ACKNOWLEDGEMENTS

THIS BOOK IS truly a collaborative effort. I am indebted to many people for its existence.

First and foremost, I am grateful to the staff at the NGOs where I worked and visited around the world from 1991 to 2020. Without their engagement, input, and ideas, I never would have had stories to share. I admire the determination and dedication of local staff to serve local residents day in and day out—my job was merely as a facilitator, catalyst, and bridge to resources. I continually learned from their tireless efforts and commitment that made and continue to make a positive difference in count-less people's lives.

In 2013, Lexi Castleman Lloyd Owen, my brilliant former assistant, suggested that she type up the large collection of correspondence that was predominantly on curled-up fax paper, almost completely faded. While overseas in the 1990s, the best way to keep in touch with my mother was via fax. That compilation then sat on a shelf until Nanor Shirikjian, my multi-talented assistant, came across it in June 2017 and thought it would make a useful resource for young people like her who might be interested in a career overseas. During the next year, she edited the faxes and transcribed my diary entries. I am indebted to both Lexi and Nanor, who thought that I had something to say. In July 2018, we toyed with the idea of a book. My thanks to kind friends who read those first writing attempts: Laurie Campbell, Célyne Darling, Polly Dolan, DeeDee Dyer, Ian Ferguson, Jill Harrington, Micki Morton, Dana Porter, Margot Porter, Helen Price, Merne

Price, Trish McMaster, and Jean Riley. Everyone was very polite, but the project lacked direction. The source material was personal and never intended for publication, and I felt diary entries and faxes just weren't that interesting. The project was shelved.

In August 2019, I was introduced to Sarah Scott, who became my publisher. After hearing a couple of stories, she suggested we chat about a book. She felt that instead of simply relating a chronology of events, the focus should be on practical tips accompanied by excerpts of stories from the field, so I thank her for figuring out a format to present the information in an accessible manner.

Appreciation goes to the next batch of obliging readers: Nahlah Ayed, Polly Benje, Diane Blake, Lily Crane-Newman, Merijn Mazzocchi, Yossi Mekelberg, Georgia Scott, and Bonnie Wims. I am forever grateful to brutally honest feedback from my brother, Ted Gibson, when I went down a rocky road, which led me to start over. For substantive feedback on a new outline, my thanks go to Barbara Becker, Susan Crane, Polly Dolan, and Kim Wilson. I am grateful to my Philanthropy Workshop Agora 2 members for their encouragement—in particular to Michelle Yue and Clare Mathias, who provided me with useful on-the-ground information. Thanks to Nicole Young, who tracked down the *60 Minutes* interview with Professor Yunus. Many thanks to generous readers who read various versions in whole or in part: Fritz Affolter, Christiane Altenburg, Kassaga Arinaitwe, The Revd Charlotte Bannister-Parker, David Bornstein, Trixie Brenninkmeijer, Brinley Bruton, Camille Cunningham, Pascale Dhombres, Sidee Dlamini, Nicky Falconer, Alexandra Fischer, Sherri Freedman, Emmanuel Gignac, Kathleen Godfrey, Beccy Goodhart, Ghada Jiha, Wanjiku

Kibui, Reda Maamari, Elissa McCarter-LaBorde, Els Malcolm, Donna Marsh, Mary-Ann Metrick, Ioana Miller, Laura Mosedale, Alexandra Murphy, Kennedy Odede, Elisabeth Paulson, Regan Ralph, Sanj Srikanthan, Aditi Thorat, Monique Villa, Caren Wakoli, Martine Van de Velde, Catherine Zennström, and, again, Diane B., Laurie C., Susan C., Polly D., Micki M., Trish McM., and Kim W.

I owe a special debt of gratitude to Becky Tinsley and Lorri Stein for their ongoing, never-failing positive reinforcement—they read every word and kept cheering me on.

Thanks to my writing coach, Rosalind de Aragues, without whose sessions the book would still be mostly in my head. My editor, Eleanor Gasparik, worked wonders revising and polishing my words. Thanks go to Tracy Bordian, my patient production editor who skillfully and efficiently led me through the process of turning the manuscript into a book, and to Sarah Miniaci, my proactive publicist.

In recent years, sharing my passion for travel and the NGO world with my son, Alexander, has been a joy. His enthusiasm, kind-heartedness, and openness will serve him well.

Finally, I am enormously thankful to my steadfast husband, Mark Bergman, who is a very attentive editor and who has been unwavering in his support of this book. Over the years, he has respected my exuberant spirit and never-ending desire to go to the field, with the exception of taking Alexander when he was a toddler to Kabul in 2004 (which I didn't). Without a doubt, someday we'll get to Afghanistan.

INDEX

ABOUT THE AUTHOR

Susan Gibson with Nobel Peace Prize Laureate Muhammad Yunus at Canada House, London, UK, on 3 March 2015. Photo courtesy Amanda Clay.

Susan Gibson has been working and volunteering in the non-profit world — for NGOs, UN agencies, and donor governments — for more than 35 years in 70 countries. She is a philanthropist actively engaged in NGOs in areas of refugees, human rights, and education for girls. She lives in Washington, D.C.